ITALIAN COOKING

Marshall Cavendish

Picture Credits:
Barry Bullough 13.
John Bulmer 2/3.
Camera Press 14.
Alan Duns 15, 17, 27, 29, 40.
Robert Harding Associates/John G. Ross 1.
Paul Kemp 49, 50, 54, 64.
Max Logan 60.
Roger Phillips 4, 5, 7, 8, 9, 10, 19, 21, 22, 25, 26, 32,
35, 36, 39, 42, 45, 52, 57, 61, 62.
Iain Reid 31, 47, 58.

Cover: Roger Phillips.

Written and edited by Isabel Moore

Published by
Marshall Cavendish Books Limited
58 Old Compton Street,
London W1V 5PA

© Marshall Cavendish Limited 1973, 1974, 1975, 1977, 1982, 1983

Parts of this material first published by Marshall
Cavendish Limited in the partwork *Supercook*

First printing 1977
Second printing 1982
Third printing 1983

Printed and bound by Graficromo Cordoba, Spain

ISBN 0 85685 247 3

Contents

An Italian farm family eats a quick picnic lunch during harvesting.

court of Catherine de Medici (who married the French King Henry II), who laid the foundations of modern French *haute cuisine*.

There are, of course, strong regional influences, and since Italy did not become one nation until the nineteenth century, each has developed individually for a lot longer than they have evolved together. In the South, in Sicily, conquered in turn by the Greeks, Carthaginians, Arabs and Normans and ruled over by Hapsburgs, Bourbons and even Bonapartes, the influence of the invaders can still be seen: there is a dish called cuscusu which is recognizably a version of the North African couscous.

The Sicilians are generally given credit for inventing pasta, with which Italian cuisine is almost synonymous, but the art of drying it and preserving it was originally Neapolitan and, not surprisingly, so are many of the most famous of the pasta sauces. Pizza, which now threatens to rival even pasta in popularity outside Italy, started life as a sort of modest,

primitive bread snack with a topping, and although versions of it are found from Sicily in the south to Genoa in the north, its home remains Naples.

Rome is the heart and soul of Italy and its cooking is renowned throughout the world. Its specialities are legion, from abbacchio (baby lamb—they are supposed to be not more than a month old when killed) to young tender artichokes called carciofi, fresh in spring, cooked in oil and not to be missed. The ancient tradition is continued with some of the wines, one of which, Falerno, can be traced back to classical times. Another, Est! Est!! Est!!!, which originated in Montefiascone near Rome, is reputed to have been popularized in the Middle Ages by a Bishop of Augsburg. Frascati, an excellent white wine, is grown in the area around the city, and is one of the carafe wines of Rome.

Tuscany to the north of Rome is where the Renaissance blazed in all its glory, and it is now the home of Italian cattle farming. Its

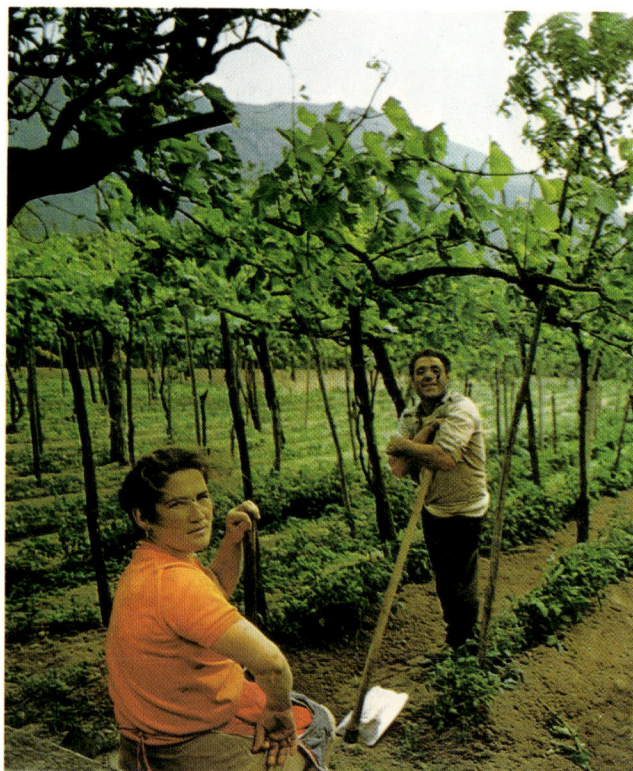

Introduction

Italy was described by a nineteenth century Mrs. Beeton as having no specially characteristic article of food. And so the uninformed have dismissed it ever since—and thus denied themselves some marvellous meals. It was not, in fact, until the recent upsurge in tourism permitted many people to visit Italy and by necessity to eat its food, that it became obvious that there was a bit more to Italian cooking than oily tomato sauces and endless varieties of pasta. When these first tourists came back, stomachs intact and palates fairly tingling with all the good things they had tasted, the word began to spread: Italian food was superb, varied—AND inexpensive.

It took a long time for the message to sink in, for the Italians were fine cooks long before they were Italians; the ancient Romans were rather famous for their feasts, and their greed was so legendary that they had the dubious distinction of inventing the vomitorium in order to indulge themselves fully. It may have said negative things about their character, but it was probably an excellent reference for their cooks!

The classical Romans are also credited with producing one of the very first cook books. It is attributed to the nobleman and gourmet, Apicius, and is positively crammed with good advice: how to turn red wine into white (according to Apicius you add egg whites and stir and stir and stir), how to make 'bad' honey 'good'. (Honey, in fact, was one of the most indispensable ingredients in those early kitchens for not only was it included in many of their sauces but it was also widely used as a preservative.)

Although Apicius' book was written in the first centuries AD, the version which survives was not published officially until the late fifteenth century—significantly, for the Renaissance saw not only a resurgence of interest in the arts and learning, but also in food and cooking. The great ruling families of the city states patronized not only the Leonardos and Michelangelos, but also countless anonymous chefs, who evolved a cuisine second to none in the world of their time. Even the French reluctantly concede that it was the Italian cooks attached to the everything!) and the tradition again is one of excellence.

In the north-west the tradition changes again: in Piedmont, proximity to France and Switzerland has meant that these two countries have influenced both the cultural and eating habits of the people. There is a local version of fondue, called fonduta, and the truffle reigns supreme, for the truffle of Piedmont is both cheaper than its Périgord cousin and less of an acquired taste. The wines cultivated around the great lakes region are particularly good and they travel well so that they can be appreciated outside their native habitat—Barbera, Barolo and the Italian answer to Champagne, Asti Spumante.

Lombardy is the rice bowl of Italy and here risottos are more popular than pasta and soups are nearly as popular as risottos (zuppa pavese is said to have been created for the French King Francis I in a peasant's hut near Milan). Saffron is one of the characteristics of local cooking ('gilding' food was considered to be health-giving in the Middle Ages and saffron was as near as the poor could get to gold) and butter is said to have been invented here and its edible potential first appreciated (the ancient Romans, apparently, used to smear it over their bodies as a sort of war paint).

Venice and Genoa owed a good deal of their early wealth and pre-eminence to their geographical position—as sea ports they were among the first to sample the produce and particularly the spices of the orient. The Venetians are especially proud of their contribution to Italian cuisine in general and to table manners in particular (they are reputed to have introduced the fork as an eating implement) and it was their eager cooks who first converted shiploads of maize from the newly discovered Americas into polenta, now a staple of the Venetian diet. In Genoa a stuffed pasta, called ravioli, was invented and, as was usually the case, other areas rapidly recognized a good idea when they saw it, adopted, adapted, called it by another name and claimed it for their own (and so the noodle is variously referred to in different parts of Italy as tagliatelle, fettuccine, tagliolini or trenette).

All in all, there's more than several things for everyone in Italian cooking—the variety is endless, the tastes delightful and, with an increasing number of delicatessens and supermarkets selling what were once esoteric Italian products, it is becoming easier—and more economical—to recreate the Italian taste in your own kitchen.

cooking therefore veers to the excellent but simple—bistecca alla fiorentina, a succulent grilled (broiled) steak exemplifies the style and also the substance of Tuscan cooking. Tuscany is also the home of Italy's best known wine, Chianti and, although it can vary wildly in quality, the Chianti Classico (distinguished by its hallmark, the black cockerel) which is produced within a legally defined area between the cities of Florence and Siena, is excellent in quality.

Emilia-Romagna is also rich in history and the city of Bologna has the reputation of having the finest restaurants in the whole country, with the possible exception of Rome. Bologna is the home of the mortadella sausage, one of the delicatessen splendours of the country, and also of a rather piquant red wine called Lambrusco which is unique in that it is supposed to be served slightly chilled. And very good it is too, when complementing the rich food of the city. Nearby Parma has its ham and cheese (served grated on practically

Soups and Antipasto

Two more delicious soups —Zuppa di Cozze (Mussel Soup) and Zuppa di Fagioli Fiorentina (Bean and Macaroni Soup).

Minestrone—the most famous of Italian soups. It is a filling mixture of beans, vegetables, macaroni and herbs and, served with crusty bread, is a meal in itself.

MINESTRONE (Vegetable and Pasta Soup)

	Metric/U.K.	U.S.
Water	900ml/ 1½ pints	3¾ cups
Dried kidney beans	125g/4oz	⅔ cup
Dried chick-peas	50g/2oz	⅓ cup
Salt pork, cubed	175g/6oz	6oz
Olive oil	50ml/2floz	4 Tbs
Medium onions, chopped	2	2
Garlic clove, crushed	1	1
Medium potatoes, diced	2	2
Carrots, sliced	4	4
Celery stalks, sliced	4	4
Small cabbage, finely shredded	½	½
Medium tomatoes, blanched, peeled, seeded and chopped	6	6
Chicken stock	2½l/4 pints	10 cups
Bouquet garni	1	1
Salt and pepper to taste		
Fresh peas, weighed after shelling	225g/8oz	1⅓ cups
Macaroni	125g/4oz	4oz
Parmesan cheese, grated	50g/2oz	½ cup

Bring the water to the boil over high heat. Add the beans and chick-peas and boil for 2 minutes. Remove from the heat and set aside to soak for 1½ hours.

Return the pan to high heat and bring to the boil again. Reduce the heat to low and simmer the beans for 1½ hours, or until they are almost tender. Drain the beans and peas in a colander and set aside.

Fry the salt pork cubes in a saucepan until they resemble small croûtons and have rendered most of their fat. Transfer the salt pork to a plate. Add the oil to the saucepan and stir in the onions and garlic. Fry until the onions are soft. Stir in the potatoes, carrots and celery and fry for 5 minutes, then add the cabbage and tomatoes. Cook for a further 5 minutes.

Pour over the stock, then add the bouquet garni, reserved beans and chick-peas, salt pork and salt and pepper. Bring to the boil, reduce the heat to low and simmer the soup for 35 minutes. Uncover and remove and discard the bouquet garni. Add the fresh peas and macaroni and cook for a further 10 to 15 minutes, or until the macaroni is 'al dente', or just tender.

Pour the soup into serving bowls and sprinkle over the grated Parmesan before serving.

8 Servings

ZUPPA DI COZZE (Mussel Soup)

	Metric/U.K.	U.S.
Olive oil	2 Tbs	2 Tbs
Medium onion, grated	1	1
Celery stalk, chopped	1	1
Garlic cloves, crushed	2	2
Salt and pepper to taste		
Dried basil	1 tsp	1 tsp
Dried oregano	$\frac{1}{2}$ tsp	$\frac{1}{2}$ tsp
Tomatoes, blanched, peeled, seeded and chopped	700g/1$\frac{1}{2}$lb	1$\frac{1}{2}$lb
Dry white wine	175ml/6floz	$\frac{3}{4}$ cup
Water	300ml/10floz	1$\frac{1}{4}$ cups
Mussels, scrubbed	2l/2$\frac{1}{2}$ pints	3 pints
Parsley, chopped	2 Tbs	2 Tbs

Heat the oil in a large saucepan. Add the onion, celery and garlic and fry until the vegetables are soft. Stir in the seasoning and herbs and cook for a further 1 minute. Stir in the tomatoes and cook for 5 minutes.

Pour over the wine and water and bring to the boil. Reduce the heat to low and simmer the mixture for 10 minutes, or until the tomatoes become pulpy. Add the mussels and cook over moderate heat, shaking the pan occasionally, for about 10 minutes, or until the shells open. (Discard any shells that do not open.) Transfer the mussels from the pan and remove and discard the top shell. Transfer the mussels to a large, warmed tureen and keep hot.

Strain the soup into a bowl, pressing on the vegetables with the back of a wooden spoon to extract all the juice. Return the strained soup

to the pan and bring to the boil. Cook for 2 minutes, then pour over the mussels. Sprinkle over the parsley and serve at once.

4 Servings

ZUPPA DI FAGIOLI FIORENTINA (Bean and Macaroni Soup)

	Metric/U.K.	U.S.
Dried white haricot (dried white) beans, soaked overnight in cold water and drained	275g/10oz	1⅔ cups
Large macaroni, broken into 10cm/4in pieces	125g/4oz	4oz
Bacon, chopped into 2½cm/1in pieces	450g/1lb	1lb
Large onion, grated	1	1
Large garlic clove, crushed	1	1
Medium tomatoes, quartered	4	4
Vegetable stock	1¾l/3 pints	7½ cups
Bouquet garni	1	1
Salt and pepper to taste		
Button mushrooms, finely chopped	50g/2oz	½ cup
Finely chopped parsley	2 Tbs	2 Tbs

Put all the ingredients, except the parsley, into a large saucepan and bring to the boil, stirring frequently. Reduce the heat to low and simmer for 1½ to 2 hours, or until the beans are cooked through. Taste the soup and adjust the seasoning if necessary.

Transfer to a warmed tureen, sprinkle over the parsley and serve at once.

6 Servings

ZUPPA DI FONTINA (Bread and Cheese Soup)

	Metric/U.K.	U.S.
Butter	75g/3oz	6 Tbs
French or Italian bread	12 slices	12 slices
Fontina cheese	12 slices	12 slices
Boiling beef stock	1¾l/3 pints	7½ cups

Melt the butter in a heavy-bottomed saucepan. Add the bread slices and fry for 3 to 4 minutes on each side, or until they are golden brown and crusty. Remove the slices from the pan and drain on kitchen towels.

Preheat the oven to moderate 180°C (Gas Mark 4, 350°F).

Arrange the bread slices in an ovenproof tureen or individual bowls and arrange a slice of cheese over each one. Pour over the stock and put the tureen or bowls into the oven. Cook for 10 minutes, or until the cheese has melted.

Remove from the oven and serve at once.

4 Servings

INSALATA DI POMODORI E SALAME (Tomato and Salami Salad)

This is one of the simplest and one of the most typical of Italian antipasto dishes. Serve with lots of crusty bread to mop up the sauce, and some mellow Chianti Classico wine.

	Metric/U.K.	U.S.
Tomatoes, thinly sliced	½kg/1lb	1lb
Salami, thinly sliced	175g/6oz	6oz
Black olives, chopped	6	6
Olive oil	6 Tbs	6 Tbs
White wine vinegar	3 Tbs	3 Tbs
Lemon juice	1 tsp	1 tsp
Large garlic clove, crushed	1	1
Salt and pepper to taste		
Chopped fresh basil	1 Tbs	1 Tbs

Arrange the tomato and salami slices in a serving dish. Separate the rows with the chopped olives.

Combine all the remaining ingredients, except the basil, in a screw-top jar and shake well to blend. Pour the dressing over the tomato mixture.

Chill in the refrigerator for 15 minutes. Sprinkle over the chopped basil before serving.

6 Servings

Fagioli al Tonno is an unusual mixture of beans and tuna fish with a tart dressing. It is usually served as an antipasto.

CAPONATA (Augergines [Eggplants] in Sweet and Sour Sauce)

This superbly aromatic dish comes from Sicily and is usually served as an hors d'oeuvre, although it can be served as an accompaniment to cold meats as well. If possible, use a good-quality vinegar, otherwise the blend of flavours will not be so delicate.

	Metric/U.K.	U.S.
Olive oil	125ml/4floz	½ cup
Small aubergines (eggplants), chopped and dégorged	4	4
Celery stalks, finely chopped	4	4
Large onions, finely chopped	4	4
Tomato purée (paste)	125g/4oz	½ cup
Water	50ml/2floz	¼ cup
Capers	1 Tbs	1 Tbs
Green olives, chopped	50g/2oz	½ cup
Red wine vinegar	75ml/3floz	⅜ cup
Sugar	1 Tbs	1 Tbs

Heat three-quarters of the oil in a large frying-pan. Add the aubergine (eggplant) dice and fry for 8 to 10 minutes, stirring occasionally, or until they are soft and brown. Remove the dice from the pan and transfer them to drain on kitchen towels.

Add the remaining oil to the pan. Stir in the celery and onions and fry until they are soft. Blend the tomato purée (paste) and water together and stir the mixture into the vegetables. Reduce the heat to low and simmer the mixture, covered, for 15 minutes. Stir in all the remaining ingredients, then return the aubergine (eggplant) dice to the pan and stir to blend thoroughly. Simmer the mixture for 20 minutes.

Transfer the caponata to a serving bowl. Chill in the refrigerator for 2 hours before serving.

4-6 Servings

FAGIOLI AL TONNO (Beans with Tuna Fish)

Beans are something of a local speciality in Tuscany and they are cooked and served in many different and very appetizing ways. This sturdy dish is now popular all over Italy—and beyond as well. Although it is served in Italy as an antipasto, with crusty bread and a mixed salad, it also makes an excellent light summer luncheon dish.

	Metric/U.K.	U.S.
Canned white haricot (white) beans, drained	450g/1lb	1lb
Medium onion, finely chopped	1	1
White wine vinegar	½ Tbs	½ Tbs
Olive oil	2 Tbs	2 Tbs
Lemon juice	1 tsp	1 tsp
Garlic clove, crushed	1	1
Salt and pepper to taste		
Chopped fresh basil	2 Tbs	2 Tbs
Canned tuna fish, drained and coarsely flaked	200g/7oz	7oz
Black olives, stoned (pitted)	6	6

Put the beans and onion into a medium serving dish. Put the vinegar, oil, lemon juice, garlic, seasoning and basil into a screw-top jar and shake vigorously to blend. Pour the dressing over the beans and onions and toss gently to blend.

Arrange the tuna fish and olives on top and serve at once.

4 Servings

Pasta, Pizze and Risotti

CANNELLONI CON RICOTTA
(Pasta Stuffed with Ricotta and Ham)

	Metric/U.K.	U.S.
Cannelloni tubes	350g/12oz	12oz
Parmesan cheese, grated	50g/2oz	½ cup
SAUCE		
Olive oil	2 Tbs	2 Tbs
Large onion, finely chopped	1	1
Garlic cloves, crushed	2	2
Canned peeled tomatoes	700g/1½lb	1½lb
Tomato purée (paste)	1 Tbs	1 Tbs
Dried basil	1½ tsp	1½ tsp
Salt and pepper to taste		
FILLING		
Ricotta cheese	225g/8oz	8oz
Thick cooked ham, diced	2 slices	2 slices
Egg	1	1
Salt and pepper to taste		

First make the sauce. Heat the oil in a sauce-pan. Add the onion and garlic and fry until the onion is soft. Stir in the tomatoes and can juice, tomato purée (paste), basil and salt and pepper, and bring to the boil. Reduce the heat to low and simmer the sauce for 30 minutes, or until it is smooth and thick.

Meanwhile, cook the cannelloni tubes in boiling, salted water for 10 to 12 minutes, or until 'al dente', or just tender. Using a slotted spoon, transfer the tubes to a large plate.

Mix all the filling ingredients together until they are thoroughly blended. Using a small teaspoon, carefully stuff the filling into the tubes until they are well filled. Arrange the tubes in a well-greased shallow ovenproof casserole.

Preheat the oven to moderate 180°C (Gas

Cannelloni con Ricotta is one of those superb pasta dishes that is technically served before the main meat dish but, in fact, can make a filling main meal in itself. The filling is rich and the sauce light, and the overall result is very appetizing indeed.

Mark 4, 350°F).

Pour the tomato sauce over the tubes and sprinkle over the grated Parmesan. Put the casserole into the oven and bake for 30 minutes, or until the top is browned and bubbling.

Serve at once.

4 Servings

FETTUCCINE ALLA BOLOGNESE (Noodles with Bolognese Sauce)

Bologna is one of the gastronomic centres of Italy, and ragu bolognese is probably one of its most notable contributions to Italian cuisine. The fettuccine which traditionally is served with it, is supposed to have been created in honour of the marriage of Lucretia Borgia to the Duke of Farrara.

	Metric/U.K.	U.S.
Fettuccine	½kg/1lb	1lb
Butter	25g/1oz	2 Tbs
Parmesan cheese, grated	50g/2oz	½ cup
RAGU BOLOGNESE Butter	25g/1oz	2 Tbs
Olive oil	1 Tbs	1 Tbs
Lean ham, finely chopped	125g/4oz	4oz
Medium onion, finely chopped	1	1
Carrot, finely chopped	1	1
Celery stalk, finely chopped	1	1
Minced (ground) beef	225g/8oz	8oz
Chicken livers, cleaned and chopped	125g/4oz	4oz
Canned peeled tomatoes, drained	425g/14oz	14oz
Tomato purée (paste)	3 Tbs	3 Tbs
Dry white wine	150ml/5floz	⅝ cup
Chicken stock	300ml/10floz	1¼ cups
Dried basil	1 tsp	1 tsp
Bay leaf	1	1
Salt and pepper to taste		

First make the ragu. Melt the butter with the oil in a saucepan. Add the ham and vegetables and fry, stirring and turning occasionally, until the vegetables are brown. Stir in the minced (ground) beef and fry until it loses its pinkness. Add all the remaining ingredients and bring to the boil, stirring occasionally. Reduce the heat to low, cover the pan and simmer the ragu for 1 hour, or until it is very thick and smooth. Remove the bay leaf. (For an extra smooth finish, the sauce may be puréed in a blender.)

Meanwhile, cook the fettuccine in boiling, salted water for 5 to 7 minutes, or until 'al dente', or just tender. Drain the fettuccine in a colander, then transfer to a warmed, deep serving bowl. Add the butter and, using two large spoons, toss gently until the butter melts.

Pour over the ragu and serve at once, with the grated cheese.

4-6 Servings

FETTUCCINE CON PROSCIUTTO (Noodles with Ham)

	Metric/U.K.	U.S.
Fettuccine	½kg/1lb	1lb
Butter	50g/2oz	4 Tbs
SAUCE Prosciutto, cut into thin strips	125g/4oz	4oz
Lean cooked ham, cut into strips	50g/2oz	2oz
Garlic sausage, cut into thin strips	175g/6oz	6oz
Large tomatoes, blanched, peeled, seeded and chopped	3	3
Dried basil	1 tsp	1 tsp
Salt and pepper to taste		

Cook the fettuccine in boiling, salted water for 5 to 7 minutes, or until 'al dente', or just tender.

Mix together the prosciutto, ham, garlic sausage, tomatoes, basil and seasoning.

Drain the fettuccine in a colander, then transfer to a warmed, deep serving bowl. Add the butter and, using two large spoons, toss gently until the butter melts.

Stir in the ham mixture until the pasta is thoroughly coated and served at once.

4-6 Servings

The variations on pasta are endless, and each one seems more exciting than the last. Noodles, particularly, come in many shapes and forms and can be made very simply into almost 'instant' meals—as here with Fettuccine con Prosciutto.

LASAGNE (Pasta Sheets with Beef and Cheese Filling)

	Metric/U.K.	U.S.
Olive oil	50ml/2floz	¼ cup
Lasagne	½kg/1lb	1lb
Mozzarella cheese, sliced	½kg/1lb	1lb
Ricotta cheese	½kg/1lb	1lb
Parmesan cheese, grated	125g/4oz	1 cup
SAUCE		
Olive oil	50ml/2floz	¼ cup
Large onions, chopped	2	2
Garlic cloves, crushed	2	2
Minced (ground) beef	1kg/2lb	2lb
Canned tomato sauce	425g/14oz	14oz
Canned peeled tomatoes	700g/1½lb	1½lb
Tomato purée (paste)	75g/3oz	3oz
Salt and pepper to taste		
Sugar	2 tsp	2 tsp
Dried basil	1 tsp	1 tsp
Bay leaves	2	2
Mushrooms, sliced	225g/8oz	2 cups

First prepare the sauce. Heat the oil in a large saucepan. Add the onions and garlic and fry until the onions are soft. Stir in the beef and cook until it loses its pinkness. Stir in all the remaining sauce ingredients, except the mushrooms, and bring to the boil. Reduce the heat to low and simmer the sauce for 2 hours, stirring occasionally. Stir in the mushrooms and simmer for a further 30 minutes. Remove and discard the bay leaves.

Meanwhile, half-fill a large saucepan and pour in half the oil. Bring to the boil over high heat. Add half the lasagne, sheet by sheet, and cook for 12 to 15 minutes, or until 'al dente', or just tender. Remove the sheets from the pan with tongs, being careful not to tear them. Add the remaining oil to the pan and cook the remaining lasagne in the same way.

Preheat the oven to moderate 180°C (Gas Mark 4, 350°F).

Put a layer of pasta over the bottom of a large, deep ovenproof casserole. Cover with a layer of meat sauce, then with alternating layers of Mozzarella, ricotta and Parmesan cheese. Continue making layers in this way until all the ingredients have been used up, ending with a layer of pasta sprinkled liberally with Parmesan.

Put the casserole into the oven and bake for 45 minutes. Serve at once.

6-8 Servings

SPAGHETTI ALLA CARBONARA (Spaghetti with Bacon and Egg Sauce)

This is one of the most popular—and most delicious—of all pasta dishes. Although the eggs are added to the pasta mixture raw, the heat will 'cook' them slightly.

	Metric/U.K.	U.S.
Spaghetti	½kg/1lb	1lb
Butter	40g/1½oz	3 Tbs
Lean bacon, chopped	125g/4oz	4oz
Double (heavy) cream	3 Tbs	3 Tbs
Eggs	3	3
Parmesan cheese, grated	125g/4oz	1 cup
Salt and pepper to taste		

Cook the spaghetti in boiling, salted water for 10 to 12 minutes, or until 'al dente', or just tender.

Meanwhile, melt one-third of the butter in a frying-pan. Add the bacon and fry until it is crisp. Remove from the heat and stir in the cream. Set aside.

Beat the eggs and half of the grated cheese together until they are well blended. Stir in salt and pepper to taste.

Drain the spaghetti in a colander then transfer to a warmed, deep serving bowl. Add the remaining butter and, using two large spoons, toss gently until the butter melts. Stir in the bacon mixture and toss gently until the spaghetti is well coated. Finally, pour over the egg mixture and toss gently until the spaghetti is well coated.

Serve at once, with the remaining grated cheese.

4-6 Servings

SPAGHETTI COL PESTO (Spaghetti with Basil and Pine Nut Sauce)

This is the great dish of the city of Genoa, which claims to grow better sweet basil than any other city in Italy! The pasta traditionally used in Genoa are trenette or egg noodles, but spaghetti has been substituted here because trenette are difficult to obtain outside Italy. Fresh basil MUST be used if the full flavour of this dish is to be preserved, but walnuts may be substituted for the pine nuts if you prefer.

	Metric/U.K.	U.S.
Spaghetti or other pasta	½kg/1lb	1lb
Butter	25g/1oz	2 Tbs
PESTO SAUCE		
Garlic cloves, crushed	2	2
Finely chopped fresh basil	50g/2oz	1 cup
Finely chopped pine nuts	3 Tbs	3 Tbs
Salt	½ tsp	½ tsp
Pepper to taste		
Olive oil	250ml/8floz	1 cup
Parmesan cheese, grated	50g/2oz	½ cup

Cook the spaghetti in boiling, salted water for 10 to 12 minutes, or until 'al dente', or just tender.

Meanwhile, crush the garlic, basil, pine nuts and salt and pepper together in a mortar until the mixture forms a smooth paste. Gradually pound in the oil, then the cheese, until the sauce is thick and smooth.

Drain the spaghetti in a colander then transfer to a warmed, deep serving bowl. Add the butter and, using two large spoons, toss gently until the butter melts. Pour the sauce over the pasta and, using the spoons, toss the ingredients gently until the pasta is thoroughly coated.

Serve at once.

4-6 Servings

Spaghetti alla Carbonara is an unlikely combination of pasta, bacon, eggs, cream and grated Parmesan cheese and it is one of the glories of the cuisine. Serve with some red wine, salad and crusty bread for a superb—and inexpensive—meal or serve, as the Italians do, as a prelude to a light meat dish, such as Scaloppine al Limone (page 32).

BASIC PIZZA DOUGH

Pizza originated in Naples but has now spread, not only to the other regions of Italy, but all over the world—there's scarcely a city of any size, anywhere, that doesn't boast a pizzeria, or other pizza eating place.

Pizza originated in Naples but its popularity is now world-wide. Pizza Margherita is a rather patriotic variation on the theme since it incorporates the colours on the Italian flag (tomatoes representing red, Mozzarella cheese representing white and chopped fresh basil for the green).

	Metric/U.K.	U.S.
Fresh yeast	15g/½oz	1 Tbs
Sugar	¼ tsp	¼ tsp
Lukewarm water	125ml/4floz plus 3 tsp	½ cup plus 3 tsp
Flour	225g/8oz	2 cups
Salt	1 tsp	1 tsp

Crumble the yeast into a small bowl and mash in the sugar. Add the 3 teaspoons of water and cream the mixture together. Set aside in a warm, draught-free place for 15 to 20 minutes, or until the mixture is puffed up and frothy.

Sift the flour and salt into a large, warmed bowl. Make a well in the centre and pour in the yeast mixture and remaining lukewarm water. Using a spatula or wooden spoon, gradually draw the flour into the liquid. Continue mixing until the flour is incorporated and the dough comes away from the sides of the bowl.

Turn out on to a lightly floured board and knead for 10 minutes. The dough should be elastic and smooth. Rinse and dry the bowl and return the dough to it. Cover with a damp cloth and set the bowl in a warm, draught-free place. Leave for 45 minutes to 1 hour, or until the dough has risen and almost doubled in bulk.

Turn the risen dough on to the floured surface and knead it for a further 3 minutes.

The dough is now ready for use.

225g/8oz dough (enough for 2 medium pizze)

PIZZA MARGHERITA (Pizza with Tomatoes and Cheese)

This delicious dish was created to honour Queen Margherita, Queen of Italy and is a patriotic combination of the colours on the Italian flag (red = tomatoes, white = Mozzarella and green = basil). Dried basil may be used if fresh is unavailable.

	Metric/U.K.	U.S.
Basic pizza dough	225g/8oz	8oz
FILLING		
Tomatoes, thinly sliced	6	6
Mozzarella cheese, sliced	175g/6oz	6oz
Chopped fresh basil	2 Tbs	2 Tbs
Salt and pepper to taste		
Olive oil	2 tsp	2 tsp

Preheat the oven to very hot 230°C (Gas Mark 8, 450°F).

Cut the pizza dough in half and roll out each piece into a circle about ½cm/¼in thick. Arrange the circles, well spaced apart, on a well greased baking sheet. Arrange the tomato slices in decorative lines over each circle, and separate them with overlapping Mozzarella slices. Sprinkle the basil generously over the top and season to taste. Dribble over the olive oil.

Put the baking sheet into the oven and bake for 15 to 20 minutes, or until the dough is cooked through and the cheese has melted.

Serve at once.

2-4 Servings

PIZZA NAPOLETANA (Pizza with Tomatoes, Cheese and Anchovies)

This is the classic Neapolitan version of pizza.

	Metric/U.K.	U.S.
Basic pizza dough	225g/8oz	8oz
FILLING		
Tomato purée (paste)	3 Tbs	3 Tbs
Medium tomatoes, blanched, peeled, seeded and chopped	4	4
Mozzarella cheese, sliced	225g/8oz	8oz
Anchovy fillets, halved	8	8
Pepper to taste		
Dried oregano	1 tsp	1 tsp
Olive oil	2 tsp	2 tsp

Preheat the oven to very hot 230°C (Gas Mark 8, 450°F).

Cut the pizza dough in half and roll out each piece into a circle about ½cm/¼in thick. Arrange the circles, well spaced apart, on a well greased baking sheet. Spoon half the tomato purée (paste) on to each circle and spread it out. Decorate each circle with half the tomatoes, cheese and anchovy fillets and sprinkle over pepper to taste and half the oregano. Dribble over the olive oil.

Put the baking sheet into the oven and bake for 15 to 20 minutes, or until the dough is cooked through and the cheese has melted.

Serve at once.

2-4 Servings

Pizza Napoletana, with its delicious topping of tomatoes, cheese and anchovies, is one of the basic, traditional pizze of Naples.

Pizza Quattrostagione has a more complicated topping—it is divided into quarters and each one is garnished with distinctive mixtures.

PIZZA QUATTROSTAGIONE
(Four Seasons Pizza)

This pizza is more elaborate than most and isn't really economical unless you are making it for at least 6 people.

	Metric/U.K.	U.S.
Basic pizza dough	450g/1lb	1lb
BASE TOPPING		
Cheddar cheese, grated	225g/8oz	2 cups
Parmesan cheese, grated	50g/2oz	$\frac{1}{2}$ cup
TOMATO TOPPING		
Tomatoes, blanched, peeled, seeded and chopped	$\frac{1}{2}$kg/1lb	1lb
Dried basil	$\frac{1}{2}$ tsp	$\frac{1}{2}$ tsp
Anchovy fillets, cut into strips	6	6
Black olives, halved and stoned (pitted)	24	24
ARTICHOKE TOPPING		
Prosciutto, halved	6 slices	6 slices
Canned artichoke hearts, drained and sliced	175g/6oz	6oz
SHRIMP TOPPING		
Mozzarella cheese, sliced	175g/6oz	6oz
Shrimps, shelled	175g/6oz	6oz
Canned asparagus tips, drained and chopped	175g/6oz	6oz
Salt and pepper to taste		
MUSHROOM AND PEPPERONI TOPPING		
Mushrooms, sliced and sautéed for 3 minutes in 25g/1oz (2 Tbs) butter	125g/4oz	1 cup
Pepperoni sausage, cut into 1cm/$\frac{1}{2}$in lengths	175g/6oz	6oz
Olive oil	1$\frac{1}{2}$ Tbs	1$\frac{1}{2}$ Tbs

Preheat the oven to very hot 230°C (Gas Mark 8, 450°F).

Divide the pizza dough into seven pieces and set one piece aside. Roll out the remaining pieces into a circle about $\frac{1}{2}$cm/$\frac{1}{4}$in thick. Arrange the circles, well spaced apart, on well greased baking sheets. Top each circle with equal amounts of grated Cheddar and Parmesan cheese.

Roll out the remaining piece of dough to a rectangle and divide into long strips, about $\frac{1}{2}$cm/$\frac{1}{4}$in wide by about 20cm/8in long. Use these strips to divide the pizze into quarters.

On one quarter of each pizza, place the tomato topping, sprinkling the tomatoes with basil, then scattering anchovies and olives on top. On the second quarter, arrange the prosciutto and artichoke slices and on the third the Mozzarella slices, in overlapping layers. Cover the cheese slices with shrimps and asparagus, and salt and pepper to taste. Arrange the mushrooms and pepperoni pieces on the fourth quarter. Dribble over the oil.

Put the baking sheets into the oven and bake for 15 to 20 minutes, or until the dough is cooked through and the cheese has melted.

Serve at once.

6 Servings

PIZZA PEPPERONI (Pizza with Sausage)

If you cannot obtain pepperoni sausage, chorizo, garlic or any type of hot Italian sausage will be just as good.

	Metric/U.K.	U.S.
Basic pizza dough	225g/8oz	8oz
Olive oil	2 tsp	2 tsp
FILLING		
Olive oil	2 Tbs	2 Tbs
Small onion, sliced	1	1
Garlic clove, crushed	1	1
Canned peeled tomatoes	425g/14oz	14oz
Salt and pepper to taste		
Tomato purée (paste)	2 Tbs	2 Tbs
Dried oregano	1 tsp	1 tsp
Bay leaf	1	1
Mozzarella cheese, sliced	175g/6oz	6oz
Pepperoni sausage, thinly sliced	1	1

First make the filling. Heat 2 tablespoons of the oil in a saucepan. Add the onion and garlic and fry until the onion is soft. Stir in the tomatoes and can juice, salt and pepper, tomato purée (paste), half the oregano and the bay leaf, and bring to the boil. Reduce the heat to low and simmer for 30 minutes, or until the sauce is thick. Remove the bay leaf.

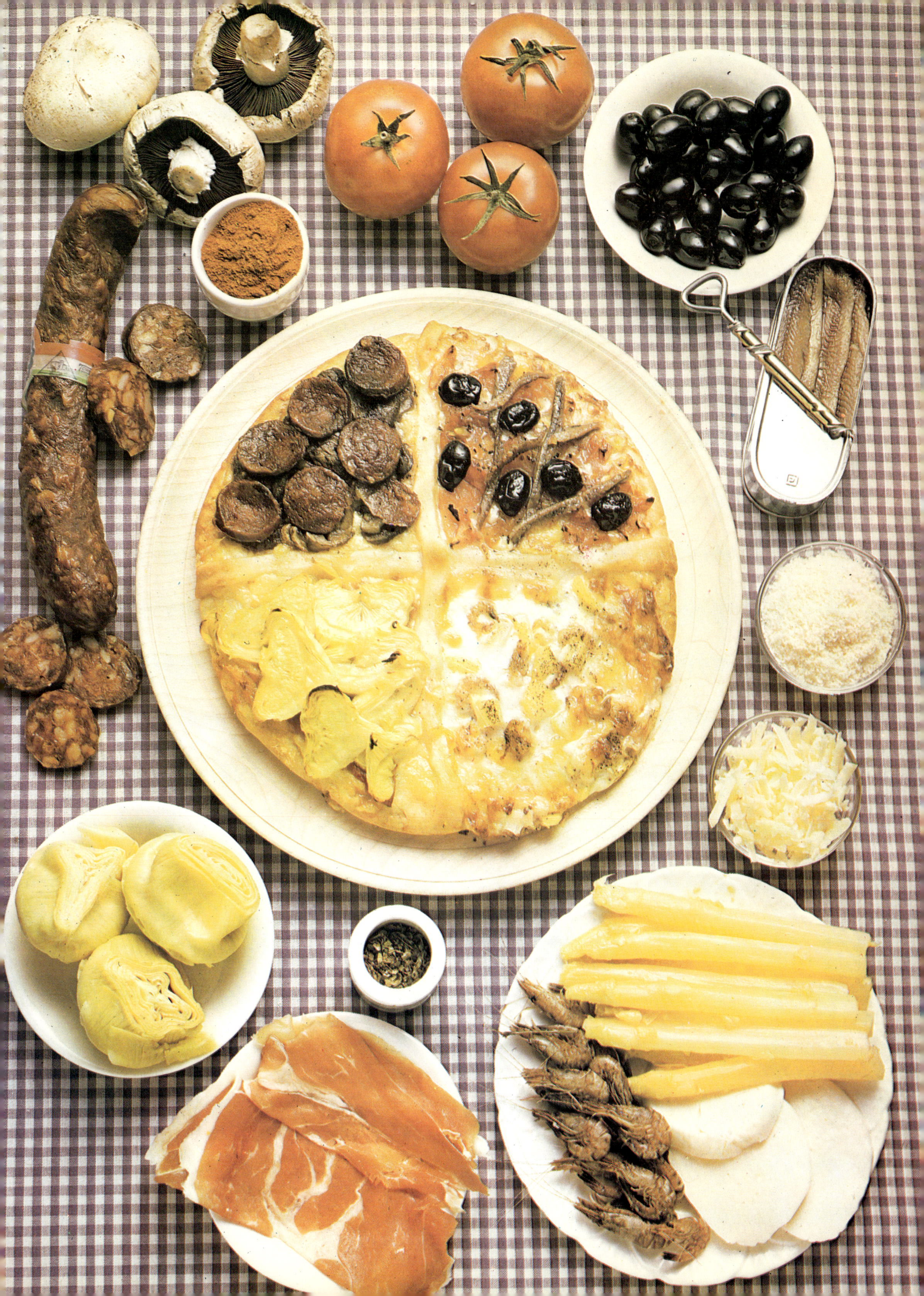

Rice is one of the staples of Italian cooking and in fact in parts of northern Italy it is more popular than pasta. To make a truly authentic risotto, Italian rice such as Avorio or Crystalo should be used, and the resulting dish will be creamier than long-grain rice and slightly nutty to taste. The two dishes pictured on the right are Risi e Bisi, a popular Venetian risotto and Risotto alla Bolognese, a combination of rice, ham and Bolognese sauce.

Preheat the oven to very hot 230°C (Gas Mark 8, 450°F).

Cut the pizza dough in half and roll out each piece into a circle about ½cm/¼in thick. Arrange the circles, well spaced apart, on a well greased baking sheet. Spoon the sauce over the dough and arrange the cheese slices on top. Sprinkle over the remaining oregano and arrange the pepperoni slices over the top. Dribble over the remaining olive oil.

Put the baking sheet into the oven and bake for 15 to 20 minutes, or until the dough is cooked through and the cheese has melted.

Serve at once.

2-4 Servings

GNOCCHI DI POLENTA (Corn Meal Dumplings with Mushroom and Ham Sauce)

Polenta is one of the staple foods of northern Italy, particularly the regions of Lombardy and Veneto. It is used in a variety of ways, including gnocchi as here.

	Metric/U.K.	U.S.
Milk	900ml/ 1½ pints	3¾ cups
Corn meal	175g/6oz	1 cup
Egg	1	1
Parmesan cheese, grated	125g/4oz	1 cup
SAUCE		
Butter	25g/1oz	2 Tbs
Small onion, chopped	1	1
Cooked ham, finely chopped	50g/2oz	½ cup
Button mushrooms, sliced	125g/4oz	1 cup
Canned peeled tomatoes	425g/14oz	14oz
Red wine	125ml/4floz	½ cup
Salt and pepper to taste		
Dried rosemary	1 tsp	1 tsp

Bring the milk to the boil, then sprinkle over the corn meal. Cook for 30 minutes, stirring constantly, or until the meal is thick. (If the meal thickens before 30 minutes, continue to cook for that time, stirring constantly to prevent it from sticking to the pan.) Stir in the egg and grated cheese.

Rinse a baking sheet with water, then turn out the mixture on to the sheet and smooth out the top (the mixture should be about 1cm/½in thick). Chill in the refrigerator for 30 minutes.

Meanwhile, to make the sauce, melt half the butter in a saucepan. Add the onion and ham and cook until the onion is soft. Add the mushrooms and cook for 3 minutes. Stir in the remaining ingredients and bring to the boil. Reduce the heat to low, cover the pan and simmer for 20 minutes.

Preheat the oven to hot 220°C (Gas Mark 6, 425°F).

Remove the mixture from the refrigerator. Cut the mixture into squares or rounds and arrange them in a well greased ovenproof dish. Cut the remaining butter into small pieces and scatter over the top. Put the dish into the oven and bake for 10 to 15 minutes, or until the top is golden brown. Serve at once.

4 Servings

RISI E BISI (Rice with Peas)

Italian rice tastes different from any other type of rice—and it's cooked differently too. Don't be alarmed if, at the end of cooking time, the rice is still quite 'creamy'—it's supposed to be like that. This particular dish is one of the classic dishes of Veneto, the region around Venice.

	Metric/U.K.	U.S.
Olive oil	1 Tbs	1 Tbs
Lean bacon, chopped	175g/6oz	6oz
Butter	50g/2oz	4 Tbs
Onion, thinly sliced	1	1
Fresh peas, weighed after shelling	½kg/1lb	1lb
Italian rice	½kg/1lb	2⅔ cups
Dry white wine	75ml/3floz	⅜ cup
Boiling chicken stock	1¼l/2 pints	5 cups
Salt and pepper to taste		
Parmesan cheese, grated	125g/4oz	1 cup

Heat the oil in a large saucepan. Add the bacon and fry until it is crisp. Transfer the bacon to kitchen towels to drain.

Add 25g/1oz (2 tablespoons) of butter to the pan and melt it over moderate heat. Add the onion and fry until it is soft. Add the peas and rice to the pan, reduce the heat to low and simmer, stirring frequently, for 5 minutes. Pour over the wine and approximately one-third of the stock. Regulate the heat so that the rice is bubbling all the time. Stir the rice occasionally with a fork. When the rice swells and the liquid is absorbed, add another one-third of the stock. Continue cooking the rice in this way until it is tender and moist but still firm.

Stir in the bacon, the remaining butter, salt and pepper and grated cheese and mix well to blend. Simmer for 1 minute, stirring frequently.

Serve at once.

4-6 Servings

RISOTTO ALLA BOLOGNESE
(Braised Rice with Ham and Bolognese Sauce)

	Metric/U.K.	U.S.
Butter	125g/4oz	8 Tbs
Medium onion, thinly sliced	1	1
Parma ham, chopped	125g/4oz	4oz .
Italian rice	½kg/1lb	2⅔ cups
Dry white wine	75ml/3floz	⅜ cup
Boiling beef stock	1¼l/2 pints	5 cups
Parmesan cheese, grated	25g/1oz	¼ cup
BOLOGNESE SAUCE		
Butter	25g/1oz	2 Tbs
Lean cooked ham, chopped	50g/2oz	2oz
Small onion, chopped	1	1
Carrot, chopped	½	½
Celery stalk, chopped	1	1
Lean minced (ground) beef	125g/4oz	4oz
Chicken livers, chopped	50g/2oz	2oz
Canned peeled tomatoes, drained	225g/8oz	8oz
Tomato purée (paste)	2 Tbs	2 Tbs
Dry white wine	75ml/3floz	⅜ cup
Chicken stock	175ml/6floz	¾ cup
Dried basil	½ tsp	½ tsp
Salt and pepper to taste		

First make the sauce. Melt the butter in a large saucepan. Add the ham, onion, carrot and

celery and fry until they are soft. Stir in the beef and cook until it loses its pinkness. Add all the remaining sauce ingredients and stir well to blend. Reduce the heat to low, cover and simmer the mixture for 1 hour.

Meanwhile, make the rice. Melt 75g/3oz (6 tablespoons) of butter in a large saucepan. Add the onion and fry until it is soft. Add the ham and rice, reduce the heat to low and cook, stirring frequently, for 5 minutes. Pour over the wine and approximately one-third of the boiling stock. Regulate the heat so that the rice is bubbling all the time. Stir the rice occasionally with a fork. When the rice swells and the liquid is absorbed, add another one-third of the stock. Continue cooking the rice in this way until it is tender and moist but still firm.

Stir in the remaining butter, the bolognese sauce and grated cheese and mix well to blend. Simmer for 1 minute, stirring frequently.

Serve at once.

4-6 Servings

RISOTTO ALLA MILANESE
(Braised Saffron Rice)

As the name suggests, this dish is a speciality of the city of Milan, in northern Italy; it is the classic accompaniment to Osso Buco.

	Metric/U.K.	U.S.
Butter	50g/2oz	4 Tbs
Chopped beef marrow	2 Tbs	2 Tbs
Onion, thinly sliced	1	1
Italian rice	½kg/1lb	2⅔ cups
Dry white wine	75ml/3floz	⅜ cup
Boiling beef stock	1¼l/2 pints	5 cups
Crushed saffron threads, soaked in 1 Tbs hot water	½ tsp	½ tsp
Parmesan cheese, grated	50g/2oz	½ cup

Melt 40g/1½oz (3 tablespoons) of butter in a large saucepan. Add the marrow and onion and fry until the onion is soft. Add the rice to the pan, reduce the heat to low, and cook, stirring frequently, for 5 minutes. Pour over the wine and approximately one-third of the stock. Regulate the heat so that the liquid is bubbling all the time. Stir the rice occasionally with a fork. When the rice swells and the liquid is absorbed, add another one-third of the stock.

Continue cooking the rice in this way until it is tender and moist but still firm.

Stir in the saffron mixture, the remaining butter and the grated cheese. Simmer for 1 minute, stirring frequently.

Serve at once.

4-6 Servings

GAMBERI CON RISO (Rice with Shrimps)

	Metric/U.K.	U.S.
Butter	50g/2oz	4 Tbs
Olive oil	2 Tbs	2 Tbs
Large onion, finely chopped	1	1
Garlic clove, crushed	1	1
Medium red pepper, pith and seeds removed and chopped	1	1
Button mushrooms, chopped	125g/4oz	1 cup
Dried basil	1 tsp	1 tsp
Salt and black pepper to taste		
Italian rice	350g/12oz	2 cups
Frozen shrimps, shelled	350g/12oz	12oz
Boiling fish stock or water	900ml/ 1½ pints	3¾ cups
Parmesan cheese, grated	50g/2oz	½ cup

Melt half the butter with the oil in a frying-pan. Add the onion, garlic and pepper and fry until they are soft. Stir in the mushrooms, basil, salt and pepper and cook for 5 minutes. Add the rice, reduce the heat to low and cook, stirring frequently, for 5 minutes. Stir in the shrimps and cook for 1 minute. Add approximately one-third of the stock. Regulate the heat so that the rice is bubbling all the time. Stir the rice occasionally with a fork. When the rice swells and the liquid is absorbed, add another one-third of the stock. Continue cooking the rice in this way until it is tender and moist but still firm.

Stir in the remaining butter and the cheese and mix well to blend. Simmer for 1 minute, stirring frequently.

Serve at once.

3-4 Servings

Fish and Seafood

Trote sulla Brace is a very simple dish of grilled (broiled) trout. Serve with stuffed tomatoes and rice for a delicious meal.

TROTE SULLA BRACE
(Grilled [Broiled] Trout)

	Metric/U.K.	U.S.
Medium trout, cleaned and with the eyes removed	4	4
Salt and pepper to taste		
Garlic cloves, halved	2	2
Rosemary sprays	4	4
Olive oil	3 Tbs	3 Tbs
Lemon, cut into 8 wedges	1	1

Preheat the grill (broiler) to moderate.

Place the fish on a flat surface and rub them all over with salt and pepper. Put half a garlic clove and a rosemary spray in the cavity of each fish. Make three shallow cuts on each side and arrange the trout in the lined grill (broiler) pan.

Lightly coat the fish with the oil, then grill (broil) the fish for 5 minutes. Remove the pan from the heat and turn the fish over. Brush with the remaining oil and grill (broil) for a further 5 to 6 minutes, or until the flesh flakes easily.

Transfer to a warmed serving dish and remove the garlic and rosemary. Garnish with lemon wedges and serve at once.

4 Servings

SOLGLIOLE ALLA VENEZIANA (Sole Marinated in Wine and Vinegar)

Venice is known as the Queen of the Sea and her diet reflects this—fish is if not the most important single ingredient in Venetian cooking, then one of the most important. This is a typical dish of the region. For economy's sake, any firm-fleshed white fish fillets, such as plaice (flounder) or whiting could be substituted for the sole.

	Metric/U.K.	U.S.
Sole fillets, skinned	8	8
Flour	50g/2oz	$\frac{1}{2}$ cup
Olive oil	75ml/3floz	$\frac{3}{8}$ cup
Salt	2 tsp	2 tsp
Large onion, sliced into rings	1	1
White wine vinegar	175ml/6floz	$\frac{3}{4}$ cup
Dry white wine	175ml/6floz	$\frac{3}{4}$ cup
Garlic cloves, crushed	2	2
Fresh marjoram	1 Tbs	1 Tbs
Fresh chopped rosemary	$\frac{1}{2}$ Tbs	$\frac{1}{2}$ Tbs
Pine nuts (optional)	3 Tbs	3 Tbs

Coat the fish fillets in the flour, shaking off any excess.

Heat the oil in a large frying-pan. Add the fillets and fry for 3 minutes on each side, or until the flesh flakes easily. Transfer to kitchen towels to drain and sprinkle over the salt. Add the onion rings to the pan and fry gently until they are soft. Transfer them to kitchen towels to drain.

Pour the vinegar and wine into a saucepan and bring to the boil. Reduce the heat to low and simmer.

Transfer the fish to a shallow, earthenware dish and scatter over the onion rings. Stir the remaining ingredients into the wine and vinegar mixture, then pour over the fillets. Set aside to cool to room temperature, then chill in the refrigerator for 4 hours, basting occasionally. Serve cold.

4-6 Servings

CACCIUCCO
(Seafood Stew)

Considered to be one of the glories of Tuscan cooking, this spicy fish stew is the speciality of the port of Livorno, or Leghorn, near Florence. To be really authentic—and sensible!—serve it in soup bowls; although it is technically a 'stew' it resembles the great, thick fish soups, such as Bouillabaisse, of the Mediterranean.

	Metric/U.K.	U.S.
Olive oil	125ml/4floz	$\frac{1}{2}$ cup
Garlic cloves, chopped	2	2
Red chilli, chopped and seeds removed	1	1
Shelled shrimps	225g/8oz	8oz
Squid, skinned, cleaned and chopped	225g/8oz	8oz
Dry white wine	125ml/4floz	$\frac{1}{2}$ cup
Tomato purée (paste)	3 Tbs	3 Tbs
Water	450ml/15floz	2 cups
Salt	$\frac{1}{2}$ tsp	$\frac{1}{2}$ tsp
Cod fillet, cut into pieces	225g/8oz	8oz
Haddock, cut into pieces	225g/8oz	8oz
Italian or French bread, toasted	4 slices	4 slices
Garlic clove, halved	1	1
Chopped pimiento	2 Tbs	2 Tbs

Heat the oil in a large saucepan or flameproof casserole. Add the chopped garlic and chilli and fry until the garlic is lightly browned. Stir in the shrimps and squid, reduce the heat to low and cover. Simmer for 30 minutes, stirring occasionally.

Pour in the wine and simmer, uncovered, for a further 15 minutes. Stir in the tomato purée (paste), water and salt, and bring to the boil. Stir in the cod and haddock pieces, cover, reduce the heat to low again and simmer for 15 minutes, or until the fish flakes easily.

Meanwhile, rub the toasted bread slices with

Cacciucco is a seafood stew from Livorno, a port in Tuscany near Florence. It is a mixture of shrimps, squid and firm-fleshed white fish, all cooked in a wine and garlic sauce.

The Italians are particularly fond of deep-frying mixtures of food and have several dishes where different meats and vegetables are cooked together. This is one of the classics, Fritto Misto di Mare, where a mixture of fish and shellfish are deep-fried in batter.

the garlic halves, then arrange a slice on the bottom of four individual bowls. Pour over the hot stew, sprinkle with the pimiento and serve at once.

4 Servings

IMPANATA DI PESCE SPADA
(Swordfish with Piquant Tomato Sauce)

Swordfish fishing is one of the major industries of Sicily, and the fish is cooked in a variety of interesting ways—in stews, casseroles, or cut into steaks and grilled (broiled). Since it can be somewhat difficult to obtain outside the Mediterranean, fresh tuna steaks or even cod may be substituted, although the tastes will be quite different.

	Metric/U.K.	U.S.
Dry white breadcrumbs	75g/3oz	1 cup
Dried oregano	1 tsp	1 tsp
Salt and pepper to taste		
Eggs, lightly beaten	2	2
Swordfish steaks	4	4
Butter	50g/2oz	4 Tbs
SAUCE		
Olive oil	50ml/2floz	¼ cup
Medium onions, sliced	2	2
Garlic cloves, crushed	2	2
Canned peeled tomatoes	425g/14oz	14oz
Capers	1 Tbs	1 Tbs
Cayenne pepper	¼ tsp	¼ tsp
Salt and pepper to taste		
Black olives, chopped	40g/1½oz	⅓ cup

First make the sauce. Heat the oil in a saucepan. Add the onions and garlic and fry until the onions are soft. Stir in all the remaining ingredients, except the black olives, and bring to the boil. Reduce the heat to low and simmer the sauce for 15 minutes.

Meanwhile, combine the breadcrumbs, oregano, salt and pepper together in a bowl. Put the eggs in a second shallow bowl. Dip the swordfish steaks first in the eggs, then in the breadcrumbs, shaking off any excess.

Melt the butter in a large frying-pan. Add the steaks to the pan and fry them, turning occasionally, for 6 to 8 minutes, or until they are lightly and evenly browned.

Transfer the steaks to the tomato sauce and carefully stir in the olives. Simmer for a further 15 minutes, basting the steaks occasionally, or until the flesh flakes easily.

Transfer the mixture to a warmed serving dish and serve at once.

4 Servings

FRITTO MISTO DI MARE
(Deep-fried Fish and Shellfish)

This is one of the great classics of Italian cooking, and can be found in restaurants and trattoria all around the coast. The fish used below are merely suggestions and are among those most widely used in Italy, but of course this is one of those dishes where you can add and subtract according to availability, season—and purse!

	Metric/U.K.	U.S.
Sufficient oil for deep-frying		
Plaice (flounder) fillets, skinned and cut into strips	2	2
Whiting fillets, skinned and cut into strips	2	2
Small scallops	4	4
Large frozen prawns or shrimps, thawed and shelled but with the tails left on	225g/8oz	8oz
Parsley sprigs	8	8
Lemon, quartered	1	1
BATTER		
Flour	125g/4oz	1 cup
Salt	¼ tsp	¼ tsp
Egg yolk	1	1
Vegetable oil	1 Tbs	1 Tbs
Milk	250ml/8floz	1 cup
Egg whites	2	2

To prepare the batter, sift the flour and salt into a bowl. Make a well in the centre and put in the egg yolk and oil. Mix the egg yolk and oil together, gradually incorporating the flour, then add the milk, a little at a time. Cover the bowl and set it aside in a cool place for 30 minutes.

Beat the egg whites until they form stiff

peaks. Quickly fold the egg whites into the batter.

Fill a large deep-frying pan about one-third full with oil and heat until it reaches 190°C (375°F) on a deep-fat thermometer, or until a small cube of stale bread dropped into the oil turns light brown in 40 seconds.

Using tongs, dip the fish pieces first into the batter, then into the oil. Fry them for 3 to 4 minutes or until they are crisp and golden brown. As each piece is cooked, remove from the pan and drain on kitchen towels. Transfer to a warmed serving dish and keep hot while you fry the remaining fish.

Garnish with parsley sprigs and lemon quarters and serve at once, piping hot.

4-6 Servings

ANGUILLA ALLA FIORENTINA (Eels with Breadcrumbs)

Eels are a great favourite in all of the countries of the Mediterranean, although this simple recipe is Italian in origin. Serve with fresh vegetables and salad, and a lightly chilled white wine, such as Toscano Bianco.

	Metric/U.K.	U.S.
Flour	75g/3oz	¾ cup
Salt and pepper to taste		
Cayenne pepper	¼ tsp	¼ tsp
Paprika	½ tsp	½ tsp
Milk	2 Tbs	2 Tbs
Egg yolk	1	1
Dry white breadcrumbs	225g/8oz	2⅔ cups
Eels, skinned, washed, and cut into 7½cm/3in pieces	1kg/2lb	2lb
Butter	75g/3oz	6 Tbs
Chopped parsley	2 Tbs	2 Tbs
Lemons, quartered	2	2

Combine the flour and seasonings in a large, shallow plate. Beat the milk and egg yolk together in a saucer and, on a third, large plate, spread out the breadcrumbs.

Roll the eel pieces, first in the flour, then in the milk mixture and, finally, in the bread-crumbs, shaking off any excess.

Melt two-thirds of the butter in a large, heavy frying-pan. Add the eel pieces and fry for 10 minutes on each side, or until they are cooked through and the outside is crisp and golden brown. Transfer them to a warmed serving dish.

Add the parsley and remaining butter to the pan. Reduce the heat to low and simmer, stirring constantly, until the butter has melted. Pour over the eels and garnish with the lemon quarters before serving.

4 Servings

CALAMARI RIPIENI
(Stuffed Squid)

This strongly flavoured dish can be served either as a filling first course, or as a light main dish, with salad.

Squid is a favourite fish in all the Mediterranean countries and it frequently forms part of Italian seafood dishes. In Calamari Ripieni, squid are stuffed with a spicy mixture of breadcrumbs, grated cheese and garlic.

	Metric/U.K.	U.S.
Medium squid, cleaned and skinned with the tender parts of the tentacles reserved	6	6
Fresh breadcrumbs	3 Tbs	3 Tbs
Finely chopped parsley	2 Tbs	2 Tbs
Grated Parmesan cheese	6 Tbs	6 Tbs
Garlic cloves, crushed	2	2
Egg, lightly beaten	1	1
Olive oil	50ml/2floz	$\frac{1}{4}$ cup
Cayenne pepper	$\frac{1}{8}$ tsp	$\frac{1}{8}$ tsp
Salt and pepper to taste		
Garlic cloves, whole	4	4
Canned peeled tomatoes	425g/14oz	14oz
Dried rosemary	$\frac{1}{2}$ tsp	$\frac{1}{2}$ tsp
Dry white wine	50ml/2floz	$\frac{1}{4}$ cup

Chop the tentacles finely and put them in a bowl. Add the breadcrumbs, parsley, cheese, 1 crushed garlic clove, the egg, 1 tablespoon of oil, the cayenne and salt and pepper, and mix well. Spoon the mixture into the squid, then with a thick needle and thread, sew up the openings.

Heat the remaining oil in a large, deep frying-pan. Add the whole garlic and fry for 5 minutes. Remove and discard the garlic. Add the squid to the pan and brown on all sides. Stir in the tomatoes and can juice, remaining crushed garlic, and the remaining ingredients. Reduce the heat to low, cover and simmer gently for 25 minutes.

Transfer the squid to a warmed serving dish and remove the thread. Slice and arrange the slices on a warmed serving dish. Pour over the sauce and serve.

3-4 Servings

Meat and Poultry

STUFATINO ALLA ROMANA
(Roman Beef Stew)

This traditional Roman dish is easy to cook—and quite delicious. Cardoons, a favourite vegetable in the area around Rome, are often added.

	Metric/U.K.	U.S.
Top rump (bottom round) of beef, cut into cubes	1kg/2lb	2lb
Seasoned flour (flour with salt and pepper to taste)	50g/2oz	½ cup
Olive oil	1 Tbs	1 Tbs
Streaky (fatty) bacon, chopped	175g/6oz	6oz
Medium onion, thinly sliced into rings	1	1
Garlic cloves, crushed	2	2
Celery stalks, thinly sliced	2	2
Fresh marjoram	1 Tbs	1 Tbs
Red wine	250ml/8floz	1 cup
Beef stock	125ml/4floz	½ cup
Tomato purée (paste)	2 Tbs	2 Tbs

Coat the cubes in the seasoned flour, shaking off any excess.

Heat the oil in a large flameproof casserole. Add the bacon pieces and fry until they are crisp and have rendered all of their fat. Transfer them to kitchen towels to drain.

Add the onion, garlic and celery to the casserole and fry until the onion is soft. Add the beef cubes and fry until they are evenly browned. Stir in the marjoram and reserved bacon, and pour over the wine and stock. Bring to the boil, reduce the heat to low and simmer the stew, uncovered, for 30 minutes, or until the liquid has reduced by about half. Stir in the tomato purée (paste) and continue to simmer for a further 30 minutes, moistening the meat with a little more stock if it becomes too dry. (It should be very tender and the sauce very thick and dark by the time the stufatino is cooked.) Serve at once.

4-6 Servings

The Italians are famous for their stews called stufatos or stufatinos, and this Roman version using beef is particularly rich and delicious. Serve with potatoes and courgettes (zucchini) for a delightful meal.

BISTECCA ALLA FIORENTINA
(Grilled [Broiled] Steak)

Tuscany is the cattle raising part of Italy and it is there that the tenderest beef—and the largest steaks!—are found. Bistecca is, quite simply, the glory of Florentine cuisine. Traditionally the steaks are cooked over a charcoal grill (broiler) but if you do not have one, the grill (broiler) of a household stove is fine.

	Metric/U.K.	U.S.
T-bone steaks, cut about 2½cm/1in thick	4	4
Butter	25g/1oz	2 Tbs
Salt and pepper to taste		
Olive oil	4 Tbs	4 Tbs

Preheat the grill (broiler) to its highest setting.

Arrange the steaks on a lined grill (broiler) pan. Cut the butter into small pieces and scatter half over the steaks. Cook for 3 minutes, then turn over and scatter over the remaining butter. Cook for a further 3 minutes.

Reduce the heat to moderate and cook for a further 3 minutes on each side. This will produce rare steaks; double the cooking time for well-done. About 1 minute before the end of cooking time, rub salt and pepper over the steaks and brush them with the olive oil.

When the steaks are cooked to your liking, transfer them to individual serving plates and serve at once.

4 Servings

ABBACCHIO BRODETTATO
(Lamb with Egg Sauce)

Abbacchio is the Roman word for sucking lamb, which is considered to be one of the great delicacies of the area. Kid is sometimes substituted in this dish.

	Metric/U.K.	U.S.
Butter	25g/1oz	2 Tbs
Vegetable oil	2 Tbs	2 Tbs
Lean lamb (leg if possible), cut into cubes	1kg/2lb	2lb
Small onion, finely chopped	1	1
Garlic cloves, crushed	2	2
Chopped fresh sage	2 tsp	2 tsp
Salt and pepper to taste		
Dry white wine	175ml/6floz	¾ cup
Chicken stock	125ml/4floz	½ cup
Lemons	2	2
Egg yolks	2	2
Parsley sprigs (to garnish)		

Melt the butter with the oil in a flameproof casserole or saucepan. Add the lamb and fry until it is evenly browned. Transfer to a plate.

Add the onion and garlic to the casserole and fry until the onion is soft. Stir in the sage, seasoning, wine and stock, and bring to the boil. Return the meat to the casserole, reduce the heat to low and cover. Simmer the mixture, stirring occasionally, for 1½ hours, or until the meat is cooked through and tender.

Meanwhile, grate the rind of one of the lemons and set aside. Beat the egg yolks and juice from both lemons together until they are mixed. Stir in the rind and seasoning to taste.

Stir about 3 tablespoons of cooking liquid from the casserole into the egg yolk mixture and mix well. Whisk the mixture gently into the simmering casserole and cook gently for 1 minute, or until the sauce has thickened slightly but not curdled.

Serve at once, garnished with parsley.

4-6 Servings

COSTOLETTA DI MAIALE ALLA PIZZAIOLA
(Pork Chops in Pizzaiola Sauce)

Pizzaiola is one of the most popular sauces in Italian cuisine and, in spite of the name, is used not only as a pizza topping but as a sauce for fish, meat (particularly pork as here) and even with noodles.

	Metric/U.K.	U.S.
Pork loin chops, about 2½cm/1in thick	6	6
Salt and pepper to taste		
Vegetable oil	50ml/2floz	¼ cup
Garlic cloves, crushed	2	2
Dried basil	1 tsp	1 tsp
Dried thyme	1 tsp	1 tsp

Costolette di Maiale de Pizzaiola is a superb dish of pork chops covered with classic pizzaiola sauce, a mixture of peppers, mushrooms and tomatoes.

	Metric/U.K.	U.S.
Bay leaf	1	1
Red wine	75ml/3floz	⅜ cup
Canned peeled tomatoes, drained and chopped	450g/1lb	1lb
Tomato purée (paste)	3 Tbs	3 Tbs
Butter	40g/1½oz	3 Tbs
Medium green peppers, pith and seeds removed and chopped	3	3
Medium onion, sliced	1	1
Button mushrooms, quartered if large	225g/8oz	2 cups
Cornflour (cornstarch), blended with 1 Tbs water	1½ Tbs	1½ Tbs
Chopped parsley	1 Tbs	1 Tbs

Rub the chops with salt and pepper.

Heat the oil in a large frying-pan. Add the chops to the pan, a few at a time, and fry until they are evenly browned. Transfer them to a plate.

Pour off all but a thin film of oil from the pan. Add the garlic and herbs, and stir to mix. Pour over the wine and bring to the boil. Stir in the tomatoes and tomato purée (paste). Return the chops to the pan and baste thoroughly with the sauce. Reduce the heat to low, cover the pan and simmer for 40 minutes, basting occasionally.

About 10 minutes before the chops are cooked through, prepare the vegetables. Melt the butter in a frying-pan. Add the peppers and onion and fry until they are soft. Stir in the mushrooms and cook for a further 3 minutes.

Transfer the vegetables to the frying-pan containing the meat. Simmer, uncovered, for 15 minutes, or until the chops are cooked through and tender. Transfer the chops to a warmed serving dish. Stir the cornflour (cornstarch) mixture into the sauce and cook, stirring constantly, for 2 minutes, or until it has thickened. Remove the bay leaf.

Pour the sauce over the chops, sprinkle over the parsley.

Serve at once.

6 Servings

COSTOLETTE DI MAIALE ALLA MILANESE (Breaded Pork Cutlets)

	Metric/U.K.	U.S.
Pork cutlets, trimmed of excess fat	4	4
Lemon juice	3 Tbs	3 Tbs
Seasoned flour (flour with salt and pepper taste)	40g/1½oz	⅓ cup
Eggs, lightly beaten	2	2
Fine dry breadcrumbs	50g/2oz	⅔ cup
Parmesan cheese, very finely grated	25g/1oz	¼ cup
Butter	50g/2oz	4 Tbs
Lemon, quartered	1	1

Put the cutlets on a shallow dish and sprinkle over the lemon juice. Set aside for 10 minutes. Pat dry with kitchen towels. Dip the cutlets, one by one, in the seasoned flour, shaking off any excess.

Put the eggs in a shallow dish. Combine the breadcrumbs and grated cheese in a second dish. Dip the cutlets, first in the eggs then in the breadcrumb mixture to coat them thoroughly. Chill in the refrigerator for 15 minutes.

Melt the butter in a large frying-pan. Add the cutlets and fry for 6 to 12 minutes on each side (depending on the thickness of the cutlets), or until they are cooked through and tender.

Transfer the cutlets to a warmed serving dish and garnish with the lemon quarters before serving.

4 Servings

SCALOPPINE ALLA MARSALA
(Veal escalopes with Marsala)

Marsala is a slightly sweet, fortified wine which is produced on the island of Sicily and much used in the Italian kitchen.

Serve with fresh vegetables and salad, and a lightly chilled white wine, such as Toscano Bianco.

	Metric/U.K.	U.S.
Veal escalopes, pounded thin	4	4
Lemon juice	3 Tbs	3 Tbs
Salt and pepper to taste		
Flour	25g/1oz	¼ cup

Saltimbocca, a melt-in-the-mouth mixture of tender veal escalope, prosciutto and fresh sage, is a speciality of the city of Rome.

Butter	50g/2oz	4 Tbs
Marsala	125ml/4floz	½ cup
Beurre manié (two parts flour and one part butter blended)	1 Tbs	1 Tbs

Sprinkle the escalopes with two-thirds of the lemon juice and set aside for 30 minutes, basting occasionally. Dry on kitchen towels and rub them with salt and pepper. Dip them into the flour, shaking off any excess.

Melt the butter in a large frying-pan. Add the escalopes to the pan and fry them for 3 to 4 minutes on each side, or until they are lightly and evenly browned. Pour over the remaining lemon juice and Marsala and cook for a further 2 minutes, stirring occasionally. Stir in the beurre manié, a little at a time, until the sauce thickens.

Transfer the escalopes and sauce to a warmed serving dish.

Serve at once.

4 Servings

SALTIMBOCCA
(Veal Escalopes with Prosciutto and Sage)

In Italian, saltimbocca means literally 'jump in the mouth' which is what this classic Roman dish does, it's so good!

	Metric/U.K.	U.S.
Veal escalopes, pounded thin	4	4
Lemon juice	2 Tbs	2 Tbs
Salt and pepper to taste		
Chopped fresh sage	2 tsp	2 tsp
Prosciutto	4 slices	4 slices
Butter	50g/2oz	4 Tbs
Dry white wine	50ml/2floz	¼ cup

Sprinkle the escalopes with lemon juice and set aside for 30 minutes, basting occasionally. Dry the escalopes on kitchen towels and rub them with salt and pepper and half the sage.

Put one slice of ham over each escalope and

trim to fit. Secure them together with wooden cocktail sticks.

Melt the butter in a large frying-pan. Add the remaining sage and fry, stirring constantly, for 1 minute. Add the escalopes to the pan and fry them for 3 to 4 minutes on each side, or until they are lightly and evenly browned. Pour over the wine and cook for a further 2 minutes.

Transfer the escalopes and pan juices to a warmed serving dish and remove the cocktail sticks. Serve at once.

4 Servings

SCALOPPINE AL LIMONE
(Veal Escalopes with Lemon Sauce)

	Metric/U.K.	U.S.
Veal escalopes, pounded thin	4	4
Lemon juice	4 Tbs	4 Tbs
Salt and pepper to taste		
Butter	50g/2oz	4 Tbs
Dry white wine or chicken stock	175ml/6floz	¾ cup
Beurre manié (one part butter and two parts flour blended)	1 Tbs	1 Tbs
Large lemon, thinly sliced	1	1
Chopped parsley	1 tsp	1 tsp

Sprinkle the escalopes with 2 tablespoons of the lemon juice and set aside for 30 minutes, basting occasionally. Dry on kitchen towels and rub them with salt and pepper.

Melt the butter in a large frying-pan. Add the escalopes to the pan and fry them for 3 to 4 minutes on each side, or until they are lightly and evenly browned. Transfer them to a plate and keep hot while you make the sauce.

Pour the remaining lemon juice and wine or stock into the pan and bring to the boil, stirring constantly. Boil for 5 minutes or until the liquid has reduced slightly. Reduce the heat to moderate and return the escalopes to the pan. Cook for 1 minute. Stir in the beurre manié, a little at a time, until the sauce thickens.

Transfer to a serving dish, garnish with lemon and parsley and serve at once.

4 Servings

INVOLTINI ALLA MARITO
(Veal Escalopes Stuffed with Cheese and Herbs)

	Metric/U.K.	U.S.
Grated Parmesan cheese	4 Tbs	4 Tbs
Chopped fresh sage	1 tsp	1 tsp
Dried oregano	½ tsp	½ tsp
Salt and pepper to taste		
Veal escalopes, pounded thin	4	4
Flour	4 Tbs	4 Tbs
Butter	50g/2oz	4 Tbs
Garlic cloves, crushed	2	2
Marsala	50ml/2floz	¼ cup
Red wine	150ml/5floz	⅝ cup

Combine the grated cheese, sage, oregano and salt and pepper to taste in a small bowl. Lay out the escalopes on a flat surface and spread a little cheese mixture over each escalope. Roll up Swiss (jelly) roll style and secure with wooden cocktail sticks.

Coat the rolls in the flour, shaking off any excess.

Melt the butter in a large frying-pan. Add the garlic and fry for 1 minute, stirring constantly. Add the veal rolls and fry until they are golden brown all over. Transfer to a plate and keep hot.

Pour the Marsala and wine into the pan and bring to the boil, stirring constantly. Return the rolls to the pan. Reduce the heat to low, cover the pan and simmer for 20 minutes.

Using a slotted spoon, transfer the rolls to a warmed serving dish. Strain the pan juices over the rolls and serve at once.

4 Servings

NOCE DI VITELLO FARCITO
(Veal Stuffed with Meat)

	Metric/U.K.	U.S.
Large veal escalopes	1kg/2lb	2lb
Lemon juice	1 Tbs	1 Tbs
Olive oil	125ml/4floz	½ cup
STUFFING		
Chicken meat, cut into strips	225g/8oz	8oz

Vitello Tonnato is a classic dish of cold roast veal served with a sauce of tuna fish and mayonnaise.

	Metric/U.K.	U.S.
Calf's liver, cut into strips	50g/2oz	2oz
Cooked ham, cut into strips	75g/3oz	3oz
Medium cooking apple, peeled, cored and grated	1	1
Marsala	125ml/4floz	½ cup
Egg yolks	2	2
Salt and pepper to taste		
French beans, trimmed, blanched and drained	125g/4oz	⅔ cup

First make the stuffing. Combine the meats and apple together. Pour over the Marsala and set aside to soak for 15 minutes.

Drain the meats and apple and return them to the bowl. Add the egg yolks and seasoning, and beat well.

Preheat the oven to moderate 180°C (Gas Mark 4, 350°F).

Lay the escalopes out on a board, overlapping the edges slightly to make a 30cm/12in square. Using a meat mallet or your clenched fist, beat the edges together to form a slight seal. Sprinkle with salt and pepper and lemon juice.

Arrange one-third of the stuffing in the middle of the meat. Cover with half the French beans and cover these with another one-third of the stuffing. Repeat the layers to use up the remaining ingredients. Fold the top and bottom sides of the escalope square over the stuffing so that they just meet. Turn in the sides to make a neat parcel. Tie the meat with string in four or five places along its length and twice around its width.

Put the meat in a roasting pan. Pour over the oil and place the pan in the oven. Roast the meat for 1 hour, or until a skewer inserted into the centre passes easily through the stuffing.

Remove from the oven, remove the meat from the pan and transfer to a warmed serving platter. Remove and discard the string and serve at once.

6-8 Servings

VITELLO ALLA PIEMONTESE
(Veal with Truffles)

	Metric/U.K.	U.S.
Veal escalope	1x700g/1½lb	1x1½lb
Veal escalope	1x½kg/1lb	1x1lb
Prosciutto, thinly sliced	125g/4oz	4oz
Pork fat, cut into thin strips	50g/2oz	2oz
Carrots, cut lengthways into thin strips	3	3
Salt and pepper to taste		
Liver sausage	175g/6oz	6oz
Truffle, finely chopped	1	1
Small green pepper, pith and seeds removed and cut into thin strips	½	½
Butter	50g/2oz	4 Tbs
Shallots, chopped	6	6
Marsala	175ml/6floz	¾ cup
Veal or beef stock	175ml/6floz	¾ cup
Beurre manié (one part butter and two parts flour blended)	1 Tbs	1 Tbs

Slice both the escalope pieces through the centre crosswise to within 1cm/½in of the end of the meat. Pull apart and lay flat on a working surface. Cover the meat with a layer of greaseproof or waxed paper and pound for 2 to 3 minutes or until the meat is slightly thinner. Remove the paper and trim the edges to neaten them. On the larger piece place the prosciutto, pork fat and carrots, and season with salt and pepper. Lay the smaller piece on top, then spread over the liver sausage. Arrange the truffle and pepper lengthways down the centre and roll up Swiss (jelly) roll style, tying firmly with string at about 2½cm/1in intervals.

Preheat the oven to moderate 180°C (Gas Mark 4, 350°F).

Melt the butter in a large flameproof casserole. Add the shallots and fry until they are soft. Add the meat and fry until it is evenly browned. Pour over the Marsala and stock and bring to the boil. Cover and transfer the casserole to the oven. Cook for 1 to 1¼ hours, or until the veal is cooked through and tender. Remove from the oven and transfer the meat to a warmed serving dish. Untruss and keep hot while you finish the sauce.

Bring the cooking liquid to the boil, then boil briskly for 5 minutes, or until it has reduced slightly. Reduce the heat to low and stir in the beurre manié, a little at a time, until the sauce thickens and becomes smooth.

Pour into a warmed sauceboat and serve at once, with the meat.

6 Servings

VITELLO TONNATO
(Cold Veal with Tuna Fish Sauce)

	Metric/U.K.	U.S.
Boned leg or loin of veal	1x1½kg/3lb	1x3lb
Anchovy fillets, halved	3	3
Garlic cloves, halved	3	3
Canned tuna fish, oil reserved	200g/7oz	7oz
Medium onion, sliced	1	1
Carrots, sliced	2	2
Veal or chicken stock	300ml/10floz	1¼ cups
Dry white wine	175ml/6floz	¾ cup
White wine vinegar	3 Tbs	3 Tbs
Bay leaves	2	2
Dried basil	1 tsp	1 tsp
Chopped parsley	1 Tbs	1 Tbs
Salt and pepper to taste		
SAUCE		
Mayonnaise	125ml/4floz	½ cup
Hard-boiled egg yolks, strained	2	2
Double (heavy) cream, stiffly beaten	3 Tbs	3 Tbs
GARNISH		
Capers	2 tsp	2 tsp
Green or black olives, halved and stoned (pitted)	6	6

Preheat the oven to moderate 180°C (Gas Mark 4, 350°F).

Put the veal on a working surface and make six incisions in the meat. Insert half an anchovy fillet and half a garlic clove in each incision. Transfer the veal to a large flame-proof casserole and add the tuna fish with its oil, the vegetables, stock, wine, vinegar, herbs and seasoning. Mix well and bring to the boil. Cover and transfer the casserole to the oven. Cook for 1½ to 1¾ hours, or until the veal is cooked through and tender. Remove from the oven and set aside to cool in the casserole.

Remove the veal from the casserole and put it on a carving board. Carve into thin slices, then arrange the slices, slightly overlapping, on a large serving dish. Set aside.

Strain the casserole liquids into a bowl, rubbing the fish, vegetables and flavourings through with the back of a wooden spoon. Pour off all but 250ml/8floz (1 cup) of the

liquid, then beat in the mayonnaise, strained egg yolks and cream until the sauce is smooth. Taste and add more seasoning if necessary.

Pour the sauce over the veal slices to cover them and carefully cover the dish with foil or greaseproof or waxed paper. Chill in the refrigerator for 8 hours, or overnight.

Remove from the refrigerator and remove the covering. Garnish with the capers and olives and serve at once.

6-8 Servings

OSSOBUCO
(Stewed Veal Knuckle or Shank)

Ossobuco is one of the great dishes of Milan, although it is now found throughout Italy. The gremolada, a spicy mixture of lemon rind, garlic and parsley, is a specifically Milanaise addition to the dish. When you put the veal pieces into the casserole, try to arrange them in one layer if possible, so that they will retain the marrow in the centre. It is traditionally served with Risotto alla Milanese.

	Metric/U.K.	U.S.
Veal knuckle or shank, sawn into 7½cm/3in pieces	1kg/2lb	2lb
Seasoned flour (flour with salt and pepper to taste)	75g/3oz	¾ cup
Butter	125g/4oz	8 Tbs
Large onion, thinly sliced	1	1
Canned peeled tomatoes	425g/14oz	14oz
Tomato purée (paste)	4 Tbs	4 Tbs
Dry white wine	175ml/6floz	¾ cup
Salt and pepper to taste		
Sugar	1 tsp	1 tsp
GREMOLADA		
Finely grated lemon rind	1 Tbs	1 Tbs
Garlic cloves, crushed	2	2
Finely chopped parsley	1½ Tbs	1½ Tbs

Dip the veal pieces in the seasoned flour, shaking off any excess.

Melt the butter in a very large, shallow flameproof casserole. Add the veal pieces and fry until they are lightly and evenly browned. Transfer them to a plate.

Add the onion to the casserole and fry until it is soft. Stir in the tomatoes and can juice and the tomato purée (paste), and cook for a further 3 minutes. Pour over the wine, salt, pepper and sugar and bring to the boil.

Return the veal pieces to the casserole and stir well. Reduce the heat to low, cover the casserole and simmer the veal for 2 to 2½ hours, or until the meat is almost falling off the bone.

Meanwhile, to make the gremolada, combine all the ingredients. Stir the gremolada into the veal mixture and cook for a further 1 minute.

Serve at once, straight from the casserole.

6 Servings

FRITTO MISTO
(Deep-fried Meat and Vegetables)

Fritto Misto is the Italian for 'mixed fry' and that is exactly what this dish is—the Italians are very fond of this method of cooking. Almost any type of meat and/or vegetables may be used, but the ingredients used below are typically Italian.

	Metric/U.K.	U.S.
Calf's sweetbreads, soaked in cold water for 1 hour and drained	2	2
Lemon juice	1 Tbs	1 Tbs
Salt	1 tsp	1 tsp
Aubergine (eggplant), peeled, sliced and dégorged	1	1
Courgettes (zucchini), sliced and dégorged	½kg/1lb	1lb
Sufficient vegetable oil for deep-frying		
Chicken breasts, boned and cut into strips	4	4
Medium mushrooms	8	8
Lemons, quartered	2	2
BATTER		
Flour	125g/4oz	1 cup
Salt	¼ tsp	¼ tsp
Eggs, lightly beaten	2	2
Vegetable oil	1 Tbs	1 Tbs
Milk	250ml/8floz	1 cup

To prepare the batter, sift the flour and salt into a bowl. Make a well in the centre and put in the

Ossobuco is a rich stew of veal knuckle or shanks and white wine. It originated in Milan although it is now popular throughout the country. Traditionally it is served with Risotto alla Milanese (page 20).

eggs and oil. Mix the eggs and oil together, gradually incorporating the flour, then add the milk, a little at a time. Cover and keep in a cool place for 30 minutes.

Put the sweetbreads in a saucepan and pour over enough water to cover. Add the lemon juice and salt. Bring to the boil, reduce the heat to moderate and cook for 15 minutes. Remove from the heat and drain the sweetbreads in a colander. Rinse well under cold running water. Carefully remove and discard the outer membrane, then cut out the tubes and any gristle. Cut the sweetbreads into 2½cm/1in cubes.

Dry the aubergine (eggplant), courgettes (zucchini) and sweetbreads with kitchen towels.

Preheat the oven to very cool 140°C (Gas Mark 1, 275°F). Line a large baking dish with kitchen towels.

Fill a large deep-frying pan one-third full with oil and heat until it reaches 190°C (375°F) on a deep-fat thermometer, or until a small cube of stale bread dropped into the oil turns golden in 40 seconds.

Using tongs, dip the chicken strips first into the batter, then carefully lower into the oil. Fry for 5 minutes. Transfer the pieces to the baking dish and keep hot in the oven.

Dip the aubergine (eggplant), courgettes (zucchini), mushrooms and sweetbread pieces into the batter and then into the oil. Fry for 2 to 3 minutes each and keep hot while you finish frying.

Transfer the fritto misto to a warmed serving dish and garnish with the lemon quarters.

Serve at once.

8 Servings

FEGATO ALLA VENEZIANA
(Calf's Liver with Onions)

This is one of the classic dishes of the Veneto, although it is now found all over Italy. The calf's liver should be cut very thinly if possible. If you can't obtain calf's liver (or can't afford it—it tends to be a luxury item in most budgets these days) lamb's liver, again very thinly sliced and cut into strips, may be substituted.

	Metric/U.K.	U.S.
Butter	25g/1oz	2 Tbs
Olive oil	2 Tbs	2 Tbs

Large onions, thinly sliced into rings	3	3
Calf's liver, thinly sliced then cut into strips	700g/1½lb	1½lb
Salt and pepper to taste		
Chopped parsley	1 Tbs	1 Tbs

Melt the butter with the oil in a large, deep frying-pan. Add the onions, reduce the heat to low and simmer, stirring occasionally, for 15 to 20 minutes, or until they are very soft.

Meanwhile, rub the liver strips with salt and pepper. Add the strips to the pan, raise the heat to moderate and fry them for 4 to 6 minutes, turning them occasionally or until they are just cooked through and tender.

When all the liver has been cooked, transfer the liver and onions to a warmed serving dish and sprinkle over the parsley.

Serve at once.

6 Servings

FEGATO DI VITELLO AL POMODORO
(Calf's Liver with Tomatoes, Mushrooms and Onions)

	Metric/U.K.	U.S.
Calf's liver, thinly sliced	700g/1½lb	1½lb
Lemon juice	3 Tbs	3 Tbs
Butter	75g/3oz	6 Tbs
Medium onions, sliced	2	2
Garlic cloves, crushed	2	2
Canned peeled tomatoes	425g/14oz	14oz
Large button mushrooms, sliced	4	4
Dried sage	1 tsp	1 tsp
Dried basil	1 tsp	1 tsp
Seasoned flour (flour with salt and pepper to taste)	25g/1oz	¼ cup

Sprinkle the liver slices with lemon juice and set them aside for 30 minutes, basting occasionally.

Melt about one-third of the butter in a saucepan. Add the onions and garlic and fry until the onions are soft. Stir in the remaining ingredients, except the seasoned flour, and bring to the boil. Reduce the heat to low, cover the saucepan and simmer the sauce for 30 minutes.

Meanwhile, dry the liver slices on kitchen towels, then dip them into the seasoned flour, shaking off any excess.

Melt the remaining butter in a large frying-pan. Add the liver slices, a few at a time, and fry them gently for 2 to 3 minutes on each side, or until they are just cooked through and tender.

When all the liver has been cooked, transfer to a warmed serving dish. Pour over the sauce and serve at once.

6 Servings

CODA DI BUE CON SEDANO
(Braised Oxtail with Celery)

This dish is particularly good if you make it the day before you plan to eat it, chill overnight in the refrigerator, then heat through.

	Metric/U.K.	U.S.
Oxtails, cut into 7½cm/3in pieces	2	2
Seasoned flour (flour with salt and pepper to taste)	50g/2oz	½ cup
Olive oil	5 Tbs	5 Tbs
Large onion, chopped	1	1

Fegato di Vitello al Pomodoro is calf's liver with tomato sauce. Serve with mashed potatoes and salad—and some good robust red wine.

Garlic cloves, crushed	2	2
Red wine	175ml/6floz	$\frac{3}{4}$ cup
Beef stock	250ml/8floz	1 cup
Canned tomatoes, drained and chopped	425g/14oz	14oz
Tomato purée (paste)	2 Tbs	2 Tbs
Bouquets garnis	2	2
Celery, chopped	1 bunch	1 bunch
Boiling water	450ml/15floz	2 cups
Cornflour (cornstarch), blended with 1 Tbs water	2 tsp	2 tsp

Preheat the oven to warm 170°C (Gas Mark 3, 325°F). Coat the oxtail pieces in the seasoned flour, shaking off any excess.

Heat half the oil in a large frying-pan. Add the oxtail pieces and fry until they are evenly browned. Transfer the pieces to a large flameproof casserole. Wipe the pan clean and pour in the rest of the oil. Add the onion and garlic and fry until the onion is soft. Pour over the wine and bring to the boil, stirring constantly. Boil until the liquid has reduced by about half. Pour the stock into the pan and cook for 2 minutes. Pour the mixture over the oxtail.

Stir the tomatoes, tomato purée (paste) and bouquets garnis into the casserole and bring to the boil. Cover and transfer to the oven. Braise for $3\frac{1}{2}$ hours.

Just before the end of the cooking period, blanch the celery pieces in boiling water for 5 minutes. Drain and stir into the casserole. Re-cover and braise for a further 30 minutes.

Remove from the oven and skim the scum from the surface. Set over moderate heat and stir in the cornflour (cornstarch) mixture. Bring to the boil and cook, stirring constantly, for 2 minutes, or until the liquid thickens and is smooth.

6 Servings

Salsicce con Fagioli is a filling casserole based on a mixture of Italian sausages and beans. It is marvellously easy to prepare and inexpensive, too.

SALSICCE CON FAGIOLI
(Sausages with Beans)

This unassuming dish is particularly good when made with a mixture of Italian hot and sweet sausages if these are available. If they are not, use ordinary beef sausages and a little garlic sausage, chopped.

	Metric/U.K.	U.S.
Dried white haricot (dried white) beans, soaked overnight and drained	450g/1lb	$2\frac{2}{3}$ cups
Water	$1\frac{1}{4}$l/2 pints	5 cups
Olive oil	2 Tbs	2 Tbs
Italian or other sausages	700g/1½lb	1½lb
Medium onions, chopped	2	2
Garlic cloves, crushed	2	2
Medium green peppers, pith and seeds removed and chopped	2	2
Canned peeled tomatoes	425g/14oz	14oz
Water	250ml/8floz	1 cup
Dried sage	1 tsp	1 tsp
Tomato purée (paste)	1 Tbs	1 Tbs
Sugar	2 tsp	2 tsp
Salt and pepper to taste		

Put the beans and water into a saucepan and bring to the boil. Reduce the heat to low and simmer the beans for 45 minutes, or until they are just tender. Drain and set aside.

Heat the oil in a flameproof casserole. Add the sausages and fry until they are lightly and evenly browned and have rendered some of their fat. Transfer to a plate and keep hot.

Pour off all but about 2 tablespoons of oil from the casserole. Add the onions, garlic and peppers and fry until they are soft. Stir in the tomatoes and can juice and water, and bring to the boil. Reduce the heat to low and cook for a further 3 minutes. Stir in all the remaining ingredients and add the beans and sausages. Reduce the heat to low and cover the pan. Simmer for 1 hour, stirring occasionally, or until the sausages are cooked through and the mixture is fairly dry.

Either serve at once or allow to cool completely and chill overnight in the refrigerator.

6-8 Servings

POLLO PARMIGIANA
(Chicken with Grated Cheese)

	Metric/U.K.	U.S.
Chicken, cut into serving pieces	1x2kg/4lb	1x4lb
Salt and pepper to taste		
Olive oil	125ml/4floz	½ cup
Mushrooms, sliced	125g/4oz	1 cup
Medium green pepper, pith and seeds removed and thinly sliced	1	1
Medium onions, sliced	3	3
Garlic, crushed	2	2
Dried oregano	1 tsp	1 tsp
Canned peeled tomatoes, chopped	425g/14oz	14oz
Dry white wine or sherry	4 Tbs	4 Tbs
Parmesan cheese, grated	75g/3oz	¾ cup

Preheat the oven to moderate 180°C (Gas Mark 4, 350°F). Rub the chicken pieces with salt and pepper and set aside.

Heat the olive oil in a large flameproof casserole. Add the chicken pieces and fry until they are evenly browned. Add the mushrooms, pepper, onions, garlic, oregano, tomatoes and can juice and wine or sherry, and bring to the boil, stirring occasionally. Cover the casserole and transfer it to the oven. Bake for $1\frac{1}{2}$ to $1\frac{3}{4}$ hours, or until the chicken is cooked through and tender.

Sprinkle one-third of the grated cheese over the top of the mixture and serve at once, with the remaining grated cheese.

4-6 Servings

BOLLITO MISTO (Boiled Chicken, Beef and Sausage)

The stock from this dish is often served as a separate soup course.

	Metric/U.K.	U.S.
Veal knuckle	1	1
Salt	1 tsp	1 tsp
Chicken	1x2kg/4lb	1x4lb
Topside (top round) of beef	1x700g/1½lb	1x1½lb
Black peppercorns	6	6
Bay leaves	2	2
Dried basil	1½ tsp	1½ tsp
Dried thyme	½ tsp	½ tsp

	Metric/U.K.	U.S.
Leeks, coarsely chopped	2	2
Celery stalks, chopped	2	2
Carrots, sliced	½kg/1lb	1lb
Small white onions, peeled and left whole	12	12
Medium white cabbage, quartered	1	1
Potatoes, sliced	1kg/2lb	2lb
Italian boiling sausage	1	1

Put the veal knuckle into a very large, heavy saucepan and half-fill the pan with water. Add the salt and bring to the boil, skimming any scum from the surface. Boil the knuckle for 45 minutes. Add the chicken, beef, peppercorns and herbs, and bring to the boil again. Reduce the heat to low, cover the pan and simmer for 1½ hours.

Add the vegetables and boiling sausage and top up the water if necessary so that it almost covers them. Bring to the boil again. Reduce the heat to low and simmer for a further 1 hour, or until the meat and vegetables are cooked through and tender. Remove and discard the veal knuckle and bay leaves. Remove the meat, chicken and sausage to a chopping board. Carve the meat into slices, the chicken into serving pieces and the sausage into bite-sized portions. Arrange them on a heated platter and surround them with the vegetables. Moisten the meat and vegetables with about 5 tablespoons of the stock and serve at once.

8-10 Servings

POLLO ALLA CACCIATORA
(Chicken with Wine, Tomatoes and Mushrooms)

	Metric/U.K.	U.S.
Butter	15g/½oz	1 Tbs
Olive oil	2 Tbs	2 Tbs
Garlic cloves, crushed	2	2
Spring onions (scallions), finely chopped	2	2
Mushrooms, sliced	175g/6oz	1½ cups
Chicken, cut into serving pieces	1x2kg/4lb	1x4lb
Salt and pepper to taste		
Dry white wine	175ml/6floz	¾ cup
Chicken stock	50ml/2floz	¼ cup

	Metric/U.K.	U.S.
Medium tomatoes, blanched, peeled, seeded and chopped	6	6
Large bay leaf	1	1
Beurre manié (one part butter and two parts flour blended)	2 tsp	2 tsp
Chopped parsley	1 Tbs	1 Tbs

Melt the butter with the oil in a flameproof casserole. Add the garlic and spring onions (scallions) and fry until they are soft. Add the mushrooms and fry for a further 3 minutes. Transfer the vegetables to a plate.

Add the chicken pieces to the casserole and fry until they are evenly browned. Stir in the seasoning, wine, stock, tomatoes, bay leaf and vegetable mixture, and bring to the boil. Reduce the heat to low, cover and simmer the mixture for 40 to 50 minutes, or until the chicken pieces are cooked through and tender. Remove from the heat and transfer the chicken pieces to a warmed serving dish. Keep hot.

Return the casserole to moderate heat and boil the sauce until it has reduced slightly. Stir in the beurre manié, a little at a time, and cook for a further 2 to 3 minutes, or until the sauce is smooth and fairly thick. Remove from the heat and discard the bay leaf.

Pour the sauce over the chicken, sprinkle over the parsley and serve at once.

4-6 Servings

POLLA ALLA BOLOGNESE
(Chicken Breasts with Ham and Cheese)

	Metric/U.K.	U.S.
Chicken breasts, skinned and boned	4	4
Seasoned flour (flour with salt and pepper to taste)	25g/1oz	4 Tbs
Butter	50g/2oz	4 Tbs
Smoked ham, thinly sliced and cut a little smaller than the chicken	8 slices	8 slices
Parmesan cheese, grated	50g/2oz	½ cup

Cut each chicken breast in half, crosswise. Place each piece between greaseproof or waxed paper and pound with a mallet to flatten.

Two superb examples of the Italian way with chicken—Pollo alla Bolognese (chicken breasts with ham and cheese) and Pollo alla Cacciatora (chicken stewed in wine, tomatoes and mushrooms).

Simplicity itself, yet so good to eat, is Pollo alla Diavolo, grilled (broiled) chicken with herbs. Serve as here, with potatoes, salad and some lightly chilled white wine for a stunning meal.

Remove from the paper and coat with the seasoned flour, shaking off any excess.

Melt half the butter in a large frying-pan. Add the chicken pieces and fry for 10 to 15 minutes, or until they are lightly and evenly browned and cooked through.

Meanwhile, melt the remaining butter in a small saucepan. Remove from the heat.

Place a slice of ham on each chicken piece and sprinkle over about one-quarter of the grated cheese. Pour over the melted butter. Return the frying-pan to moderate heat, cover and cook the mixture for 3 to 4 minutes or until the cheese has melted.

Using a slotted spoon, transfer the chicken mixture to a warmed serving dish and serve at once, with the remaining cheese.

4 Servings

POLLO ALLA DIAVOLA
(Grilled [Broiled] Chicken with Herbs)

	Metric/U.K.	U.S.
Chickens, cut in half lengthways	2x1kg/2lb	2x2lb
Large garlic clove, halved	1	1
Salt and pepper to taste		
Butter	125g/4oz	8 Tbs
Olive oil	2 Tbs	2 Tbs
Lemon juice	1 Tbs	1 Tbs
Chopped parsley	1 Tbs	1 Tbs
Dried basil	1½ tsp	1½ tsp

Preheat the grill (broiler) to moderate.

Rub the chicken halves all over with the garlic clove halves, then with salt and pepper. Discard the garlic.

Melt the butter with the oil in a small saucepan. Remove from the heat and stir in the lemon juice, parsley and basil. Brush the chicken all over with the butter and herb mixture, then place the halves, skin side down, on the lined grill (broiler) rack.

Put under the grill (broiler) and grill (broil) for 7 to 10 minutes on each side, basting frequently with the butter mixture. After 15 minutes, test the chicken for doneness by inserting a skewer into one of the thighs; if the juices run clear the birds are cooked.

Remove the chicken halves to a warmed serving dish and spoon over any remaining butter and herb mixture. Serve at once.

4 Servings

CONIGLIO AL VINO BIANCO
(Rabbit in White Wine)

	Metric/U.K.	U.S.
Water	1¾l/3 pints	7½ cups
Malt vinegar	1 Tbs	1 Tbs
Rabbit, cleaned and cut into serving pieces	1x2kg/4lb	1x4lb
Butter	50g/2oz	4 Tbs
Onions, sliced	2	2
Garlic cloves, crushed	2	2
Carrots, chopped	2	2
Celery stalks, chopped	3	3
Dry white wine	350ml/12floz	1½ cups
Dried rosemary	½ tsp	½ tsp
Dried oregano	½ tsp	½ tsp
Salt and pepper to taste		
Beurre manié (one part butter and two parts flour blended)	1 Tbs	1 Tbs

Pour the water and vinegar into a large bowl. Add the rabbit pieces and baste well. Marinate at room temperature for 8 hours, or overnight. Remove the rabbit from the bowl and discard the marinade. Pat dry with kitchen towels.

Preheat the oven to moderate 180°C (Gas Mark 4, 350°F).

Melt the butter in a flameproof casserole. Add the rabbit pieces and fry until they are evenly browned. Transfer them to a plate. Add the onions and garlic to the casserole and fry until they are soft. Add the carrots and celery and fry for 5 minutes. Pour over the wine, herbs and seasoning. Bring to the boil.

Return the rabbit pieces to the casserole and baste well. Cover and transfer the casserole to the oven. Cook for 1 to 1¼ hours, or until the rabbit is cooked through and tender.

Remove from the oven and transfer the rabbit pieces to a warmed serving dish. Keep hot while you finish the sauce. Put the casserole over high heat and bring the juices to the boil. Reduce the heat to low and add the beurre manié, a little at a time, stirring constantly until the sauce thickens. Serve at once.

6 Servings

Vegetables and Salads

ZUCCHINI RIPIENI
(Stuffed Courgettes)

	Metric/U.K.	U.S.
Dried mushrooms	15g/½oz	¼ cup
Medium courgettes (zucchini), trimmed	12	12
Fresh white breadcrumbs, soaked in 4 Tbs milk	50g/2oz	1 cup
Eggs, lightly beaten	2	2
Salt and pepper to taste		
Dried oregano	1 tsp	1 tsp
Parmesan cheese, grated	175g/6oz	1½ cups
Prosciutto, chopped	50g/2oz	2oz
Olive oil	50ml/2floz	¼ cup

Put the mushrooms in a bowl, pour over enough water to cover and soak for 30 minutes. Drain, chop and reserve.

Bring a large saucepan of salted water to the boil. Add the courgettes (zucchini) and boil for 7 to 8 minutes, or until they are just tender. Drain in a colander. Slice the vegetables in half lengthways and scoop out the flesh, taking care not to break the skins. Set aside.

Squeeze any excess moisture out of the breadcrumbs and place them in a bowl. Add the reserved courgette (zucchini) flesh, the eggs, salt, pepper, oregano, half the cheese, the prosciutto and reserved mushrooms. Mix all the ingredients together.

Preheat the oven to fairly hot 200°C (Gas Mark 6, 400°F). Lightly grease a shallow ovenproof casserole with a little of the oil. Arrange the courgette halves in the dish.

Spoon a little stuffing into each courgette (zucchini) half and sprinkle over the remaining cheese. Sprinkle over the remaining oil.

Put the casserole into the oven and bake for 20 minutes, or until the cheese has melted and the courgettes (zucchini) are golden on top. Serve at once.

6-12 Servings

Zucchini Ripieni is a dish of courgettes stuffed with breadcrumbs, ham and mushrooms, then covered with cheese. Serve with salad and crusty bread as a light snack lunch, or as a superb vegetable accompaniment to steak or chops.

FAGIOLI AL FORNO
(Tuscan Baked Beans)

Dried white haricot (dried white) beans are immensely popular in northern Italy, particularly in Tuscany, where they form part of many of the classic dishes of the area.

	Metric/U.K.	U.S.
Dried white haricot (dried white) beans, soaked overnight and drained	½kg/1lb	2⅔ cups
Garlic cloves, crushed	3	3
Chopped fresh basil	3 Tbs	3 Tbs
Salt and pepper to taste		
Ground cinnamon	½ tsp	½ tsp
Streaky (fatty) bacon, coarsely chopped	8 slices	8 slices

Preheat the oven to very cool 140°C (Gas Mark 1, 275°F).

Place the beans, garlic, basil, seasoning, cinnamon and bacon in a large ovenproof casserole. Stir and add just enough water to cover the mixture. Cover and put the casserole into the oven. Bake for 3 to 3½ hours, or until the beans are very tender but still firm.

Remove from the oven, strain off any excess liquid and serve at once.

6 Servings

CAVOLO IN AGRODOLCE
(Sweet and Sour Cabbage)

The Italians are very fond of the 'sweet and sour' taste in food, especially game and vegetables—rabbit and hare for instance and courgettes (zucchini) are also cooked in this way.

	Metric/U.K.	U.S.
Vegetable oil	50ml/2floz	¼ cup
Medium onion, chopped	1	1
Small green cabbage, finely shredded	1	1
Tomatoes, blanched, peeled, seeded and chopped	4	4
White wine vinegar	2 Tbs	2 Tbs
Salt and pepper to taste		
Sugar	1 Tbs	1 Tbs

Heat the oil in a deep frying-pan. Add the onion and fry until it is soft. Stir in the cabbage, a handful at a time, and, as it goes down, add the next. Then stir in the tomatoes, vinegar, salt and pepper. Reduce the heat to low and simmer for 15 to 20 minutes, or until the cabbage is cooked.

Stir in the sugar and cook for 1 minute longer. Transfer to a warmed serving dish and serve at once.

4 Servings

CROCCHETTINE DI PATATE
(Potato Croquettes with Cheese and Ham)

	Metric/U.K.	U.S.
Potatoes	1kg/2lb	2lb
Butter, softened	25g/1oz	2 Tbs
Eggs, lightly beaten	4	4
Parmesan cheese, grated	75g/3oz	¾ cup
Cooked ham, finely diced	50g/2oz	2oz
Salt and pepper to taste		
Grated nutmeg	½ tsp	½ tsp
Fine dry breadcrumbs	75g/3oz	1 cup
Sufficient vegetable oil for deep-frying		

Boil the potatoes in salted water for 15 to 20 minutes, or until they are tender. Drain and mash them. Transfer to a large bowl. Beat in the butter, half the beaten egg mixture, the grated cheese, ham, seasoning and nutmeg until the mixture is well blended.

Using your hands, form the mixture into sausage shapes about 5cm/2in long. Arrange on a baking sheet and chill in the refrigerator for 15 minutes.

Put the remaining beaten egg in one shallow dish and the breadcrumbs in another. Remove the croquettes from the refrigerator and dip them, one by one, first in the eggs then in the breadcrumbs, shaking off any excess.

Fill a large deep-frying pan one-third full with oil and heat until it reaches 190°C (375°F) on a deep-fat thermometer, or until a small cube of stale bread dropped into the oil turns golden in 40 seconds.

Carefully lower the croquettes into the oil, a few at a time, and fry for 3 to 4 minutes, or until they are golden brown. As they are cooked, transfer to kitchen towels to drain and

keep hot while you cook the remaining croquettes in the same way.

Serving piping hot.

4-6 Servings

MELANZANE ALLA PARMIGIANA
(Aubergine [Eggplant] Parmesan)

This delicious and filling dish is almost more popular in the United States than in its native land. In Italy, Parma ham is sometimes substituted for the Mozzarella used in this recipe, and a meat sauce (similar to ragu Bolognese) can also be substituted for tomato sauce if you wish the dish to be more substantial.

	Metric/U.K.	U.S.
Olive oil	about 175ml/ 6floz	about ¾ cup
Aubergines (eggplants), sliced and dégorged	4	4
Mozzarella cheese, sliced	175g/6oz	6oz
Parmesan cheese, grated	75g/3oz	¾ cup
SAUCE		
Olive oil	3 Tbs	3 Tbs
Medium onions, chopped	2	2
Garlic cloves, crushed	2	2
Tomatoes, blanched, peeled and chopped	½kg/1lb	1lb
Tomato purée (paste)	4 Tbs	4 Tbs
Dried basil	2 tsp	2 tsp
Salt and pepper to taste		

To make the sauce, heat the oil in a saucepan. Add the onions and garlic and fry until the onions are soft. Stir in the tomatoes, tomato purée (paste) and the remaining ingredients, and bring to the boil. Reduce the heat to low, cover the pan and simmer the sauce for 30 minutes, or until it is thick and rich. Remove from the heat.

Meanwhile, heat about 50ml/2floz (4 tablespoons) of olive oil in a large frying-pan. Add a few of the aubergine (eggplant) slices and fry until they are golden brown on both sides. Transfer them to a plate. Cook the remaining slices in the same way, adding more oil as necessary.

Preheat the oven to moderate 180°C (Gas

Mark 4, 350°F).

Arrange about one-third of the aubergine (eggplant) slices on the bottom of an ovenproof casserole. Cover with half the Mozzarella slices and a third of the sauce. Top with a generous sprinkling of grated cheese. Continue making layers in this way until all the ingredients are used up, finishing with a layer of aubergine (eggplant) slices covered with sauce and grated cheese.

Put the dish into the oven and bake for 45 minutes.

Serve at once.

4-6 Servings

PEPERONATA
(Red Pepper and Tomato Stew)

This dish is one of the classics of Italian cuisine and can be served as an accompaniment to lamb, veal or chicken.

	Metric/U.K.	U.S.
Butter	25g/1oz	2 Tbs
Olive oil	2 Tbs	2 Tbs
Large onion, thinly sliced	1	1
Garlic clove, crushed	1	1
Red peppers, pith and seeds removed and cut into strips	½kg/1lb	1lb
Tomatoes, blanched, peeled and chopped	½kg/1lb	1lb
Salt and pepper to taste		
Bay leaf	1	1

Melt the butter with the oil in a large saucepan. Add the onion and garlic and fry until the onion is soft. Stir in the red peppers, reduce the heat to low and cover. Simmer for 15 minutes. Stir in the tomatoes, seasoning and bay leaf, and simmer, uncovered, for a further 20 minutes. If there is too much liquid in the pan, increase the heat to moderately high and cook for 5 minutes, or until the mixture is thick and some liquid has evaporated.

Remove from the heat and discard the bay leaf. Serve at once, if you are serving the peperonata hot. (This dish is equally good served cold.)

4-6 Servings

Peperonata is a classic stew of red peppers and tomatoes. Serve with veal escalopes, or sliced liver.

Peppers are very popular in Italy and are incorporated into many meat dishes, as well as being served by themselves as a vegetable. In this Peperoni Ripieni, they are stuffed with a tomato, tuna, anchovy and olive mixture, and could be served as a light snack meal as well as a filling vegetable accompaniment.

PEPERONI RIPIENI
(Peppers Stuffed with Tomatoes, Tuna, Anchovies and Olives)

This dish can be served as a first course, as an accompaniment to steak dishes, or even (if you serve two per person) as a light lunch.

	Metric/U.K.	U.S.
Large green peppers	4	4
Olive oil	4 Tbs	4 Tbs
Medium onion, thinly sliced	I	I
Garlic cloves, crushed	2	2
Canned peeled tomatoes	700g/1½lb	1½lb
Tomato purée (paste)	2 Tbs	2 Tbs
Dried basil	½ tsp	½ tsp
Dried oregano	½ tsp	½ tsp
Salt and pepper to taste		
Chopped parsley	I Tbs	I Tbs
Canned tuna, drained and flaked	350g/12oz	12oz
Anchovy fillets, chopped	4	4
Black olives, chopped	6	6
Capers	2 tsp	2 tsp
Parmesan cheese, grated	25g/1oz	¼ cup

Slice off about 2½cm/1in from the wider end of each pepper. Carefully remove and discard the pith and seeds. Set aside. Remove and discard the stems from the sliced tops and chop the flesh into small dice. Set aside.

Heat half the oil in a large frying-pan. Add the onion, garlic and pepper dice and fry until the onion is soft. Stir in the tomatoes and can juice, tomato purée (paste), herbs, salt and pepper. Cover and cook, stirring occasionally, for 25 minutes, or until the mixture has thickened. Stir in the remaining ingredients, except the cheese, and cook the mixture for 5 minutes.

Preheat the oven to warm 170°C (Gas Mark 3, 325°F).

Remove from the heat and spoon the sauce into the peppers, filling them to within about 1cm/½in of the top.

Brush a baking pan with about 1 tablespoon of the remaining oil. Arrange the peppers in the pan and put the pan into the oven. Bake for 45 minutes, basting occasionally with the remaining oil. After 45 minutes, sprinkle the tops of the peppers with the grated cheese and bake for a further 15 minutes, or until the cheese is brown and bubbly. Remove from the oven and serve at once.

4 Servings

PISELLI AL PROSCIUTTO
(Peas with Prosciutto)

This dish is Roman in origin although it is found throughout Italy now. Use fresh petits pois if at all possible; frozen if necessary. It can be served as a vegetable accompaniment or as an hors d'oeuvre, with lots of crusty bread.

	Metric/U.K.	U.S.
Butter	50g/2oz	4 Tbs
Small onion, finely chopped	1	1
Fresh peas, weighed after shelling	½kg/1lb	1lb
Salt and pepper to taste		
Chicken stock	50ml/2floz	¼ cup
Prosciutto, cut into strips	175g/6oz	6oz

Melt the butter in a saucepan. Add the onion and fry until it is soft. Stir in the peas, seasoning and stock, and bring to the boil. Reduce the heat to low and simmer the peas for 8 to 10 minutes, or until they are just tender. Add the prosciutto strips and simmer the mixture for a further 3 minutes, stirring from time to time.

Transfer the contents of the pan to a warmed serving dish.

Serve at once.

4 Servings

ZUCCA ALLA PARMIGIANA
(Pumpkin, Parma-Style)

Pumpkin is a popular vegetable all over Italy and this is a particularly delicious way of cooking it. It is fairly rich, so serve with a light main dish, such as veal escalope or grilled (broiled) lamb and lots of mixed salad.

	Metric/U.K.	U.S.
Eggs, lightly beaten	2	2
Dry breadcrumbs	50g/2oz	⅔ cup
Pumpkin flesh, sliced	1kg/2lb	2lb
Butter	50g/2oz	4 Tbs
Parmesan cheese, finely grated	25g/1oz	¼ cup
SAUCE		
Olive oil	2 Tbs	2 Tbs
Onion, finely chopped	1	1
Garlic clove, crushed	1	1
Canned peeled tomatoes	425g/14oz	14oz
Tomato purée (paste)	2 Tbs	2 Tbs
Chopped fresh basil	1 Tbs	1 Tbs
Chopped parsley	1 Tbs	1 Tbs
Sugar	1 tsp	1 tsp
Salt and pepper to taste		

To make the sauce, heat the oil in a saucepan. Add the onion and garlic and fry until the onion is soft. Stir in the tomatoes and can juice, tomato purée (paste), herbs, sugar and seasoning, and bring to the boil. Reduce the heat to low and simmer the sauce for 15 minutes. Remove the pan from the heat and keep hot.

Preheat the oven to moderate 180°C (Gas Mark 4, 350°F).

Put the eggs in one dish and the breadcrumbs in another. Dip the pumpkin slices first in the eggs then in the breadcrumbs, shaking off any excess.

Melt the butter in a large frying-pan. Add the pumpkin slices, a few at a time, and fry until they are evenly browned. Transfer the slices to a well-greased ovenproof baking dish. Pour over the sauce and sprinkle over the cheese. Put the dish into the oven and bake for 30 minutes, or until the cheese is golden brown and bubbling.

Remove the dish from the oven and serve at once.

6 Servings

INSALATA DI FUNGHI
(Mushroom Salad)

	Metric/U.K.	U.S.
Olive oil	3 Tbs	3 Tbs
Lemon juice	1 Tbs	1 Tbs
Salt and pepper to taste		
Button mushrooms, thinly sliced	225g/8oz	2 cups
Cooked peas	50g/2oz	⅓ cup
Lettuce, shredded	1	1

Combine the oil, lemon juice, salt and pepper in a screw-top jar and shake to blend thoroughly.

Arrange the mushrooms and peas in a bowl and pour over the dressing. Toss thoroughly and chill in the refrigerator for at least 30 minutes.

Line a serving dish with the lettuce. Pile the mushroom mixture into the centre and serve at once.

4 Servings

FUNGHI MARINATE
(Marinated Mushrooms)

	Metric/U.K.	U.S.
Small button mushrooms, stalks removed	½kg/1lb	1lb
MARINADE		
Salt	1 tsp	1 tsp
Black peppercorns, coarsely crushed	½ tsp	½ tsp
Dried dill	1 tsp	1 tsp
Tarragon vinegar	4 Tbs	4 Tbs
Lemon juice	1 Tbs	1 Tbs
Olive oil	50ml/2floz	¼ cup

Combine all the marinade ingredients in a shallow bowl. Stir in the mushrooms and baste them with the liquid. Cover the dish and set aside in a cool place to marinate for 2 hours, basting frequently.

Drain off and discard the marinade and pile the mushrooms on a serving dish. Serve at once.

6 Servings

INSALATA D'ARANCIA
(Orange Salad)

	Metric/U.K.	U.S.
Lettuce, shredded	1 crisp	1 crisp
Oranges, peeled, pith removed and separated into segments	2	2
Large tomato, thinly sliced	1	1
Lemon juice	1 Tbs	1 Tbs
Vegetable oil	1 Tbs	1 Tbs
Chopped chives	1 tsp	1 tsp
Salt and pepper to taste		

Arrange the lettuce on a serving plate.

Put the orange segments and tomato slices in a bowl. Combine all the remaining ingredients in a screw-top jar and shake well to blend. Pour over the fruit and toss well to blend.

Arrange the fruit and dressing mixture over the lettuce and chill in the refrigerator for 15 minutes before serving.

4 Servings

INSALATA DI FINOCCHIO
(Fennel Salad)

	Metric/U.K.	U.S.
Fennel, trimmed	1 head	1 head
Chicory (French or Belgian endive), outer leaves removed	1 head	1 head
Tomatoes, thinly sliced	4	4
Olive oil	4 Tbs	4 Tbs
White wine vinegar	2 Tbs	2 Tbs
Garlic clove, crushed	1	1
Salt and pepper to taste		

Thinly slice the fennel and chicory (endive) and arrange them in a serving dish. Add the tomatoes.

Combine all the remaining ingredients in a screw-top jar and shake well to blend. Pour the dressing over the fennel mixture and toss gently to blend. Chill in the refrigerator for 30 minutes before serving.

4-6 Servings

Salads can either be accompaniments to the main dish or antipasta in Italy and these two delightful dishes are no exception : Insalata di Funghi, a refreshing mushroom and pea salad at the top, and Insalata d'Arancia, an orange and tomato salad at the bottom.

Desserts and Cakes

CILIEGE AL MARSALA
(Cherries in Marsala)

	Metric/U.K.	U.S.
Canned stoned (pitted) Morello cherries, drained	1kg/2lb	2lb
Marsala	150ml/5floz	$\frac{5}{8}$ cup
Grated nutmeg	$\frac{1}{2}$ tsp	$\frac{1}{2}$ tsp
Sugar	1 Tbs	1 Tbs
Double (heavy) cream, stiffly beaten	150ml/5floz	$\frac{5}{8}$ cup

Put the cherries, Marsala, nutmeg and sugar into a saucepan and bring to the boil, stirring until the sugar has dissolved. Reduce the heat to low and simmer gently for 10 minutes. Remove from the heat and transfer the cherries to a serving dish.

Return the pan to the heat and boil the liquid briskly for 3 to 4 minutes, or until it is thick and syrupy. Pour the syrup over the cherries.

Chill the dish in the refrigerator for at least 1 hour. Top the cherries with the cream before serving.

4 Servings

RICOTTA AL CAFFE
(Ricotta Cheese with Coffee)

Ricotta cheese is a very popular cooking ingredient all over Italy, and it is used equally in both savoury dishes, such as Lasagne (page 12) and sweet dishes such as the recipe below. If you cannot obtain ricotta, cottage cheese may be substituted.

	Metric/U.K.	U.S.
Ricotta cheese	350g/12oz	12oz
Castor (superfine) sugar	175g/6oz	$\frac{3}{4}$ cup
Freshly percolated strong black coffee	50ml/2floz	$\frac{1}{4}$ cup
Dark rum	50ml/2floz	$\frac{1}{4}$ cup
Walnuts, halved	2	2

Rub the cheese through a strainer, using the back of a wooden spoon. Beat the sugar, coffee and rum into the cheese and continue beating until the mixture is smooth and thick. Set aside at room temperature for 1 hour.

Spoon the mixture into individual serving glasses and chill in the refrigerator for 1 hour. Decorate each glass with half a walnut before serving.

4 Servings

GELATO DI PISTACCHIO
(Pistachio Ice-cream)

You will need either an ice-cream maker with paddles or a churn for this recipe. Serve with crisp wafers or, to be really authentic, little amoretti biscuits (cookies).

	Metric/U.K.	U.S.
Single (light) cream	250ml/8floz	1 cup
Pistachio nuts, shelled, chopped and blanched	125g/4oz	1 cup
Double (heavy) cream	250ml/8floz	1 cup
Almond essence (extract)	½ tsp	½ tsp
Egg yolks	3	3
Sugar	50g/2oz	¼ cup
Water	75ml/3floz	⅜ cup
Egg whites, stiffly beaten	3	3

Put the single (light) cream and nuts in a blender and blend until the nuts are puréed. Spoon the mixture into a small saucepan and stir in the double (heavy) cream. Place over low heat and simmer gently until the mixture is hot. Remove from the heat, cover and set aside to cool.

Pour the mixture into a medium-sized bowl, beat in the almond essence (extract) and set aside.

Beat the egg yolks until they are well blended.

Dissolve the sugar in the water over low heat, stirring constantly. Increase the heat to moderate and boil the syrup until the temperature reaches 140°C (220°F) on a sugar thermometer or until a little of the syrup spooned out of the pan and cooled will form a short thread when drawn out between your index finger and thumb. Remove from the heat and let the syrup stand for 1 minute.

Pour the syrup over the egg yolks in a steady stream, whisking constantly. Continue whisking until the mixture is thick and fluffy. Mix in the cooled cream mixture, then fold in the beaten egg whites.

Pour the mixture into an ice-cream container equipped with paddles or into a hand-propelled ice-cream churn, and freeze according to manufacturers' instructions.

Store in the frozen food storage compartment of the refrigerator and serve as required.

4 Servings

BUDINO DI RICOTTA
(Cheese and Almond Pudding)

	Metric/U.K.	U.S.
Butter	1 tsp	1 tsp
Fine dry breadcrumbs	1 Tbs	1 Tbs
Sultanas or seedless raisins	1 Tbs	1 Tbs
Chopped mixed candied peel	2 Tbs	2 Tbs
Rum	50ml/2floz	¼ cup
Ricotta cheese	½kg/1lb	1lb
Eggs	4	4
Ground almonds	75g/3oz	½ cup
Slivered almonds	50g/2oz	⅓ cup
Ground cinnamon	½ tsp	½ tsp
Grated lemon rind	1 Tbs	1 Tbs
Sugar	50g/2oz	¼ cup

Preheat the oven to moderate 180°C (Gas Mark 4, 350°F). Lightly grease a large baking dish with the butter, then sprinkle over the breadcrumbs.

Put the sultanas or raisins and candied peel in a small bowl. Cover with rum and set aside to soak for 10 minutes.

Using the back of a wooden spoon, rub the ricotta through a strainer into a large bowl. Beat in the eggs, then gradually add the sultana or raisin mixture and all of the remaining ingredients.

Turn the mixture into a baking dish and put the dish into the oven. Bake for 45 minutes to 1 hour, or until the top is light brown. Remove from the oven and set aside to cool. When the mixture is cold, transfer it to the refrigerator and chill for at least 1 hour.

To serve, run a knife around the edge of the dish and quickly invert the mixture on to a serving dish.

4-6 Servings

Simplicity itself, yet a deliciously satisfying dessert, is Ciliege al Marsala, cherries in Marsala.

ZABAGLIONE
(Egg Yolk and Wine Dessert)

This has rightly been called the queen of Italian desserts, and there's scarcely a self-respecting Italian housewife or restaurant chef who doesn't have at least one version of it at her fingertips. It is traditionally served warm, but if you prefer, it can be chilled in the refrigerator.

	Metric/U.K.	U.S.
Egg yolks	4	4
Castor (superfine) sugar	4 Tbs	4 Tbs
Marsala	4 Tbs	4 Tbs
Grated lemon rind	2 tsp	2 tsp

Beat the egg yolks and sugar together in a heatproof bowl until they thicken and become pale yellow. Place the bowl over a saucepan one-third full of boiling water and put the pan over moderate heat. Add the Marsala and lemon rind and continue beating until the mixture rises slightly and stiffens. Remove from the heat.

Spoon into individual serving glasses and serve at once.

4 Servings

ZUPPA INGLESE
(English Trifle)

Despite the name, this recipe is NOT a soup but a rather fanciful Italian idea of what constitutes a traditional English trifle!

	Metric/U.K.	U.S.
Sponge cakes, sliced in half crosswise	2x18cm/7in	2x7in
Marsala	250ml/8floz	1 cup
Zabaglione (make double the quantity given in the recipe above)		
Double (heavy) cream, stiffly beaten	475ml/16floz	2 cups
Maraschino cherries	16	16

Place one-half of the sponge, cut side up, on a serving plate. Sprinkle over about a quarter of the Marsala, then spread over one-third of the zabaglione. Continue making layers in this way until all the ingredients are used up, ending with a layer of sponge.

Spread the cream over the top and sides of the trifle. Arrange the cherries decoratively over the surface and chill in the refrigerator for 1 hour.

Remove the plate from the refrigerator and serve at once.

6 Servings

ZUPPA A DUE COLORI
(Two-Coloured Sponge Pudding)

This stunning dessert looks fabulous—and complicated—when it is assembled but in actual fact it is quite easy to make. It is very rich to eat, so serve after a fairly light main dish such as veal or chicken.

	Metric/U.K.	U.S.
Chocolate sponge cake, thinly sliced	2x20cm/8in	2x8in
Chocolate-flavoured liqueur	125ml/4floz	$\frac{1}{2}$ cup
Sponge cake, thinly sliced	1x18cm/7in	1x7in
Rum	125ml/4floz	$\frac{1}{2}$ cup
Thick custard	350ml/12floz	$1\frac{1}{2}$ cups
Double (heavy) cream, stiffly beaten	300ml/10floz	$1\frac{1}{4}$ cups
Dark cooking (semi-sweet) chocolate, grated	50g/2oz	2 squares
Flaked hazelnuts, toasted	125g/4oz	1 cup
CHOCOLATE CREAM		
Dark cooking (semi-sweet) chocolate, broken into pieces	$\frac{1}{2}$kg/1lb	16 squares
Butter	25g/1oz	2 Tbs
Rum	50ml/2floz	$\frac{1}{4}$ cup
Eggs, lightly beaten	5	5

First make the cream. Put the chocolate, butter and rum into a heatproof bowl placed over a pan of simmering water. Set the pan over low heat and cook, stirring constantly, until the chocolate and butter have melted. Beat in the eggs, one at a time and, beating constantly, cook the cream for 12 to 15 minutes, or until it

begins to thicken. Remove the pan from the heat and the bowl from the pan. Set the cream aside.

Place half the chocolate sponge slices in a layer on the bottom of a deep, glass serving bowl. Pour over one-half of the chocolate-flavoured liqueur. Using a flat-bladed knife, spread half the chocolate cream over the sponge. Place half the plain sponge slices over the cream and sprinkle with half the rum.

Spoon all of the custard over and continue making layers in this way, ending with the plain sponge.

Put the pudding in the refrigerator to chill for 1 hour. Remove from the refrigerator. Spoon over the cream, sprinkle with the grated chocolate and hazelnuts.

Serve at once.

8 Servings

Zabaglione is one of the glories of Italian cuisine and has carried the reputation of its excellence throughout the world. It is very easy to make, too, being a simple mixture of egg yolks, sugar, Marsala and grated lemon rind.

ZUCCOTTO
(Pumpkin-Shaped Cream and Sponge Dessert)

This rich dessert makes a superb ending to a dinner party, and can be made ahead of time, if you prefer.

	Metric/U.K.	U.S.
Double (heavy) cream, stiffly beaten	600ml/1 pint	2½ cups
Icing (confectioners') Sugar	25g/1oz plus 2 Tbs	¼ cup plus 2 Tbs
Hazelnuts, toasted	50g/2oz	½ cup
Fresh cherries, halved and stoned (pitted)	225g/8oz	2 cups
Dark dessert (semi-sweet) chocolate, chopped or grated	124g/4oz	4 squares
Brandy	50ml/2floz	¼ cup
Orange-flavoured liqueur	50ml/2floz	¼ cup
Chocolate sponge cakes, halved horizontally	2x20cm/8in	2x8in
Cocoa powder	2 Tbs	2 Tbs

Combine the cream and 25g/1oz (¼ cup) of icing (confectioners') sugar in a bowl. Fold in the hazelnuts, cherries and chocolate and chill the mixture in the refrigerator.

Mix together the brandy and orange-flavoured liqueur.

Line a 1¼l/2 pint (1½ quart) pudding basin with three-quarters of the sponge, cutting it into pieces so that it fits the shape of the basin. Sprinkle the brandy mixture over the sponge lining. Spoon the cream mixture into the sponge cake, then use the remaining sponge to cover the top. Chill the mixture in the refrigerator for 2 hours.

Remove from the refrigerator and run a knife around the edge of the pudding to loosen it. Invert a serving plate over the basin and, holding the two together, reverse them. The zuccotto should slide out easily.

Sprinkle half of the remaining icing (confectioners') sugar over one-quarter of the pudding and half the cocoa powder over a second quarter, then repeat these over the other half of the pudding so that the zuccotto has four alternating segments of colour.

Serve at once.

8-10 Servings

CASSATA ALLA SICILIANA
(Sponge Cake with Chocolate Icing)

	Metric/U.K.	U.S.
Fresh Madeira (pound) cake, about 23cm/9in long by 7½cm/3in wide	1	1
Ricotta cheese	½kg/1lb	1lb
Double (heavy) cream	2 Tbs	2 Tbs
Sugar	50g/2oz	¼ cup
Orange-flavoured liqueur	2 Tbs	2 Tbs
Chopped mixed candied fruit	2 Tbs	2 Tbs
Chopped pistachio nuts	1 Tbs	1 Tbs
Dark cooking (semi-sweet) chocolate, grated	50g/2oz	2 squares
ICING Dark cooking (semi-sweet) chocolate, cut into small pieces	350g/12oz	12 squares
Black coffee	175ml/6floz	¾ cup
Unsalted butter, cut into small pieces and chilled	225g/8oz	16 Tbs

Cut the cake, lengthways, into 1cm/½in slices.

Using the back of a wooden spoon, rub the ricotta through a strainer into a bowl, then beat until it is smooth. Beat in the cream, sugar and liqueur. Fold in the candied fruit, pistachios and grated chocolate.

Put the bottom cake slice on a flat serving plate and spread it evenly with a fairly thick layer of the ricotta mixture. Cover with another slice of cake on top and spread with the ricotta mixture. Continue making layers in this way until all the ingredients are used up, ending with a slice of cake on top. Gently press the 'loaf' together. Wrap the cake in foil and chill in the refrigerator for 3 hours, or until the filling is set and firm.

Melt the chocolate with the coffee in a small saucepan over low heat, stirring constantly. Remove from the heat and beat in the butter, a piece at a time. Continue beating until the mixture is smooth. Transfer the icing to a bowl and allow to cool until it reaches a thick, spreading consistency.

Reserve a little icing for decoration, then cover the top and sides of the cake with the remainder, swirling it on with a flat-bladed knife. Fill a piping bag with the reserved icing

Zuccotto, a classic pumpkin-shaped cream, cherry and chocolate sponge dessert.

Cassata alla Siciliana is a rich cake dessert which makes a spectacular end to any meal.

and pipe it decoratively over the top and sides.

Cover the cake loosely with foil and chill in the refrigerator for 12 hours before serving.

8-10 Servings

CROSTATA DI RICOTTA
(Cheese Cake)

	Metric/U.K.	U.S.
PASTRY		
Butter, cut into small pieces	175g/6oz	12 Tbs
Flour	225g/8oz	2 cups
Salt	$\frac{1}{4}$ tsp	$\frac{1}{4}$ tsp
Egg yolks, lightly beaten	4	4

Sugar	2 Tbs	2 Tbs
Marsala	5 Tbs	5 Tbs
Grated lemon rind	$1\frac{1}{2}$ tsp	$1\frac{1}{2}$ tsp
FILLING		
Ricotta cheese	$1\frac{1}{4}$kg/$2\frac{1}{2}$lb	$2\frac{1}{2}$lb
Sugar	125g/4oz	$\frac{1}{2}$ cup
Flour	2 Tbs	2 Tbs
Vanilla essence (extract)	$\frac{1}{2}$ tsp	$\frac{1}{2}$ tsp
Grated rind of 1 orange		
Grated rind and juice of 2 lemons		
Raisins	3 Tbs	3 Tbs
Finely chopped candied peel	2 Tbs	2 Tbs
Slivered almonds	2 Tbs	2 Tbs
Egg white, lightly beaten	1	1

Lightly grease a 23cm/9in springform pan with a little butter. Set aside.

To make the pastry, sift the flour and salt into a large bowl. Make a well in the centre and drop in the remaining butter, the egg yolks, sugar, Marsala and lemon rind. Using your fingertips, lightly combine all the ingredients, then knead the dough until it is smooth and can be formed into a ball. Do not overhandle. Cover the dough and chill in the refrigerator for about 1 hour, or until it is fairly firm.

Break off about a quarter of the dough. Dust it with flour, cover and return to the refrigerator. Reshape the rest of the dough into a ball, then flatten into a circle. Roll out to a circle about 5cm/2in wider than the pan. Using the rolling pin, gently ease the dough into the pan to form a case, trimming off any excess.

Preheat the oven to moderate 180°C (Gas Mark 4, 350°F).

To make the filling, beat all the ingredients together, except the almonds and egg white, until they are well blended. Spoon into the dough case and sprinkle over the almonds.

Remove the reserved dough from the refrigerator and roll out to a rectangle at least 25cm/10in long. Cut the dough into long strips, then arrange the strips across the filling to make a lattice pattern. Brush with the egg white.

Put the pie into the oven and bake for 1 hour, or until the crust is golden and the filling is firm to touch. Remove from the oven and transfer to a wire rack. Remove the pie from the pan and leave to cool. Serve cold, in wedges.

6-8 Servings

CENCI
(Deep-Fried Pastry Fritters)

These delightful fritters look like lovers' knots and are served as a snack, or as an accompaniment to ice-creams and fruit salads.

	Metric/U.K.	U.S.
Flour	275g/10oz	2½ cups
Icing (confectioners') sugar	1½ Tbs	1½ Tbs
Salt	½ tsp	½ tsp
Eggs	2	2
Egg yolks	2	2
Rum or red wine	2 Tbs	2 Tbs
Sufficient vegetable oil for deep-frying		

Sift 225g/8oz (2 cups) of the flour with a third of the sugar and the salt into a bowl. Make a well in the centre and pour in the eggs, egg yolks and rum or wine. Using a wooden spoon, gradually draw the flour into the liquids, stirring gently until the mixture is blended to a smooth dough. Shape into a ball.

Spread about half the remaining flour over a working surface and knead the dough in the flour for about 10 minutes, or until it is shiny. Wrap in greaseproof or waxed paper and chill in the refrigerator for 1 hour.

Sprinkle the remaining flour over the surface. Cut the dough into quarters and roll out each piece until it is paper thin. Divide the

Crostata di Ricotta, one of the original cheesecakes and still one of the best. This version has a superb pastry, flavoured with Marsala, and a filling of ricotta cheese, grated orange and lemon rind and raisins. The end result is dripping with calories but unbelievably good!

dough into strips 1cm/½in wide by 12½cm/5in long, shaping the lengths into loose knots. Set aside.

Fill a large deep-frying pan one-third full with oil and heat until it reaches 180°C (350°F) on a deep-fat thermometer, or until a small piece of stale bread dropped into the oil turns golden in 50 seconds.

Drop the knots into the oil, a few at a time, and deep-fry until they are light brown and puffed up. Transfer them to kitchen towels to drain and keep hot while you fry the remaining dough knots.

Arrange the knots on a serving dish, sprinkle over the remaining sugar and serve warm.

4 Dozen

Pandolce is a sweet bread, one of the specialities of the port of Genoa in northern Italy. Serve it warm with butter, or on its own for a tasty snack.

PANDOLCE
(Genoese Sweet Bread)

This delicious sweet bread, flavoured with pine and pistachio nuts and fennel, is the speciality of Genoa, *in northern Italy. Serve on its own or with lots of butter.*

	Metric/U.K.	U.S.
Fresh yeast	25g/1oz	1oz
Sugar	175g/6oz	¾ cup
Lukewarm milk	425ml/14floz	1¾ cups
Flour	900g/2lb	8 cups
Salt	1 tsp	1 tsp
Orange-flower water	3 Tbs	3 Tbs
Butter, melted	75g/3oz	6 Tbs
Pine nuts	50g/2oz	⅓ cup
Pistachio nuts	50g/2oz	½ cup
Raisins, soaked in 3 Tbs Marsala for 30 minutes and drained	175g/6oz	1 cup
Fennel seeds, crushed	2 tsp	2 tsp
Aniseed, crushed	½ tsp	½ tsp
Candied lemon peel,		

chopped	50g/2oz	⅓ cup
Candied citron, chopped	50g/2oz	⅓ cup
Grated rind of 1 orange		

Crumble the yeast into a bowl and mash in ½ teaspoon of sugar with a fork. Add 4 tablespoons of the milk and cream the mixture together. Set the bowl aside in a warm, draught-free place for 15 to 20 minutes or until the yeast mixture is puffed up and frothy.

Sift the flour, salt and remaining sugar into a warmed mixing bowl. Make a well in the centre and pour in the yeast mixture, the remaining milk and the orange-flower water. Add the melted butter and, using your fingers or a spatula, gradually draw the flour mixture into the liquid. Continue mixing and beating briskly until all the flour is incorporated and the dough comes away from the sides of the bowl.

Turn the dough out on to a floured board or marble slab and knead it for 10 minutes, reflouring the surface if it becomes sticky. The dough should be elastic and smooth. Rinse, dry and lightly grease the bowl. Shape the dough into a ball and return it to the bowl. Cover with a damp cloth and set aside in a warm, draught-free place for 1 to 1½ hours, or until the dough has risen and almost doubled in bulk.

Turn the risen dough on to a floured surface. Using your fingers, push out the dough until it forms a square about 1cm/½in thick. Sprinkle over the nuts, raisins, fennel seeds, aniseed, peel, citron and orange rind. Roll up the dough Swiss (jelly) roll style. Push into a square again and, using the heel of your hand, flatten it out to about 2½cm/1in thick. Roll up Swiss (jelly) roll style again.

Shape the dough into a round and arrange on a well-greased baking sheet. Return the dough to the warm, draught-free place for 1 to 1¼ hours or until it has almost doubled in bulk.

Preheat the oven to fairly hot 190°C (Gas Mark 5, 375°F).

Make three cuts in the top of the dough to make a triangular shape. Put the baking sheet into the centre of the oven and bake the bread for 20 minutes. Reduce the oven temperature to warm 170°C (Gas Mark 3, 325°F) and continue to bake the bread for a further 1 hour.

Remove the sheet from the oven. Tip the bread off the baking sheet and rap the underside with your knuckles. If it sounds hollow, like a drum, it is cooked. If it does not sound hollow, return the bread, upside-down, to the oven and bake for a further 10 minutes.

Cool completely on a wire rack before serving.

One 1¼kg/2½lb Loaf

PANETTONE
(Breakfast Bread)

This bread is a speciality of the city of Siena, in Tuscany. Serve on its own or with lots of butter.

	Metric/U.K.	U.S.
Butter, softened	75g/3oz	6 Tbs
Fresh yeast	15g/½oz	½oz
Sugar	75g/3oz	⅜ cup
Lukewarm water	50ml/2floz	¼ cup
Flour	450g/1lb	4 cups
Salt	1½ tsp	1½ tsp
Lukewarm milk	175ml/6floz	¾ cup
Eggs, lightly beaten	3	3
Candied citron, chopped	75g/3oz	½ cup
Sultanas or seedless raisins	75g/3oz	½ cup
Raisins	3 Tbs	3 Tbs
Grated lemon rind	2 tsp	2 tsp
Butter, melted	25g/1oz	2 Tbs

Using 1 tablespoon of the softened butter, grease a 1kg/2lb coffee tin or a tall cylindrical mould about 15cm/6in in diameter and about 18cm/7in high. Line with greaseproof or waxed paper greased with another 1 tablespoon of softened butter. Allow the excess paper to come up over the rim of the tin. Set the tin aside.

Crumble the yeast into a small bowl and mash in ½ teaspoon of sugar. Add the water and cream the water and yeast together. Set aside in a warm, draught-free place for 15 to 20 minutes, or until the mixture is puffed up and frothy.

Sift the flour, the remaining sugar and the salt into a large bowl. Make a well in the centre and pour in the yeast mixture and the milk. Using a spatula, gradually draw the flour into the liquids until all the flour is incorporated and the dough comes away from the sides of the bowl. Turn the dough out on to a lightly floured surface and knead for 10 minutes. The dough should be elastic and smooth.

Rinse, dry and lightly grease the mixing bowl. Shape the dough into a ball and return it to the bowl. Cover with a damp cloth and set in a warm, draught-free place for 2 hours, or until the dough has risen and almost doubled in bulk. Beat in the remaining softened butter, the eggs, citron, sultanas or seedless raisins, raisins and lemon rind until they are well blended. Re-cover the bowl and return to the warm place for a further 1 hour, or until the dough has risen slightly.

Put the dough into the prepared tin or mould. Brush the top with a little melted butter. Set aside in the warm, draught-free place for 30 minutes, or until the dough has risen slightly.

Preheat the oven to fairly hot 200°C (Gas Mark 6, 400°F). Brush the dough with a little more of the melted butter. Put the tin or mould into the oven and bake for 30 minutes. Reduce the oven temperature to moderate 180°C (Gas Mark 4, 350°F) and bake the bread for a further 30 minutes, brushing once more during the cooking time with the remaining melted butter.

Zeppole are mouth-watering doughnuts from Naples. Serve as a snack with milk or freshly percolated coffee.

Remove the bread from the oven and allow to cool in the tin for 20 minutes. Remove from the tin and transfer to a wire rack to cool, upright, until it is completely cold.

10-12 Servings

ZEPPOLE (Neapolitan Doughnuts)

These delightful little doughnuts are a speciality of the city of Naples, and are much easier to cook than most doughnuts

	Metric/U.K.	U.S.
Water	725ml/ 1¼ pints	3 cups
Salt	½ tsp	½ tsp
Sugar	50g/2oz	¼ cup
Brandy	2 Tbs	2 Tbs
Flour	350g/12oz	3 cups
Sufficient vegetable oil for deep-frying		
Icing (confectioners') sugar	50g/2oz	½ cup
Ground cinnamon	2 tsp	2 tsp

Pour the water, salt, sugar and brandy into a large saucepan. Set the pan over moderate heat and bring the mixture to the boil. Using a wooden spoon, stir in the flour until the mixture comes away from the sides of the pan. Remove from the heat and beat vigorously until the dough becomes light and elastic.

Turn out the dough on to a lightly floured surface and shape into a ball. Beat with a pestle or rolling pin for 10 minutes, reshaping it into a ball whenever it becomes flat. Divide the dough into 16 pieces and roll each one into a sausage shape about 25cm/10in long. Shape the pieces into rings and press the ends together to seal. Prick each ring with a form.

Fill a large saucepan one-third full with oil and heat until it reaches 190°C (375°F) on a deep-fat thermometer, or until a small cube of stale bread dropped into the oil turns golden in 40 seconds. Carefully lower the dough rings into the oil, a few at a time, and fry for about 5 minutes or until they are golden brown. Remove from the oil and drain on kitchen towels.

Sift the icing (confectioners') sugar and cinnamon together in a small bowl. Sprinkle over the zeppole.

16 doughnuts